COLLINS DICTIONARY OF BRIDGE TERMS

COLLINS
DICTIONARY OF
BRIDGE
TERMS

PETER DONOVAN & DAVID PARRY

CollinsWillow
An Imprint of HarperCollins*Publishers*

First published in 1991 as
The Bridge Player's Dictionary
by Mr Bridge Limited

This fully revised edition published in 1994 by
CollinsWillow
an imprint of HarperCollins*Publishers*
London

ISBN 0 00 218476 1

A CIP catalogue record for this book is
available from the British Library

Printed and bound in Great Britain by
HarperCollins Manufacturing, Glasgow

INTRODUCTION

In 1935, Ely Culbertson produced a bridge encyclopedia which was generally recognized as the authoritative source of reference to the game for the next thirty years – until the American Contract Bridge League (ACBL) sponsored *The Official Encyclopedia of Bridge**, which was published in 1964. This was a truly momentous work with one simply stated objective: 'To provide an official and authoritative answer to any question a reader might ask about contract bridge and its leading players'. The focus was naturally on the American market, where bridge was already more part of the culture than in other parts of the world. But three years later, in 1967, an 'International Edition' was published in England, entitled *The Bridge Players' Encyclopedia*. This was basically a translation of the original work and also involved the replacement of some American biographies and results with their Anglo–European counterparts; it had 674 pages and cost a mere 42 shillings (£2.10). Almost exactly another thirty years on, it would be timely for an updated edition of that excellent work to be produced, though I suspect that the gigantic nature of the task would daunt even the most ambitious of editors!

The *Collins Dictionary of Bridge Terms* is not remotely comparable to its eminent forerunners; it is a comprehensive illustrated lexicon and glossary of terms used in the game today. I believe it is the first-ever publication of its kind, with potentially a much wider appeal to a greater range of players than an encyclopedia would have.

---

* A 5th Edition has recently been published, priced $39.95

Any non-player, who hears a group of bridge enthusiasts discussing and analysing hands, will inevitably feel that he is listening to a load of gobbledegook. For, quite simply, bridge talk is a foreign language to anyone who is not familiar with the game. There is no other game in the world which uses a more obtuse, absurd and erroneous vocabulary of words and phrases than does bridge, not to mention the jargon and slang associated with them! I'm sure it's accurate to assert that the majority of players themselves are confused by much of the terminology bandied about in bridge circles, although many would be reluctant to admit it. 'Deep finesse' and 'Double squeeze' are two of the more reasonable phrases used to describe certain types of card play but, at the other extreme, 'grapes' and 'plums' have become 'new generation' jargon for the minor suits (clubs and diamonds); so there is pressing need for general clarification of bridge terminology. It is really not surprising that the media, and the general public at large, still view bridge as a complex game, confined to the upper classes, intellectuals, and raving lunatics! Wise folk know that this is far from the truth, yet very few of the game's influential devotees have done much to change its image.

A language without a dictionary is unheard of, but the bridge world has had to make do without one until now. Thanks to the resources, tenacity, and enthusiasm of a successful businessman called John Magee, a group of archivists and researchers was convened about four years ago to start collecting every known word and expression used in bridge – complete with explanations. My co-editor, David Parry, was part of the initial team and he pays particular tribute to Giles Thompson, who did the lion's share of the donkey work in compiling data and definitions. Other significant contributions were made by Simon Ainger, Dennis Cook, Eric Crowhurst, Jeremy Dhondy, Elena Jeronimidis, David Martin and Bob Rowlands. My task with David has been a difficult but pleasant one in sifting through a massive surplus of material – rejecting, refining, and re-writing items to finish up with this publication. We are both very satisfied with the result, even though we have left plenty of scope for revision in future editions!

The *Collins Dictionary of Bridge Terms* contains a clear explanation of every word and phrase which is used commonly in

British bridge, including the popular jargon and slang phrases, which are printable! Most of the technical terms are illustrated with helpful examples, so there is no need to struggle with understanding complex definitions. We have also included several biographical and historical references to individuals and organizations, which are significant to the game. Our judgement on what to include and what to leave out has been made in accordance with one of our main objectives – to produce a complete reference book of technically and socially acceptable bridge terminology. If you don't find the word you're looking for, we have probably deemed it to be 'non-U' or unprintworthy!

This dictionary is the one bridge publication for which every player will have a use. Whether it be for information, education, entertainment, or just controversy – it is tremendous value. You need no longer feel embarrassed about asking the meaning of a phrase, which others may think you ought to know. It is the ultimate handy reference book on contemporary bridge in Britain, and no teacher can afford to be without a copy. Reading it from cover to cover isn't likely to improve your game, but it will clarify many misconceptions. Its simple style and presentation will help promote the image that Bridge is actually still an easy game to learn!

P.D.

—A—

ABOVE THE LINE
Phrase used in rubber bridge to identify scores entered above the horizontal line on the score sheet arising from penalties, overtricks, premiums for slams, honours etc. which do not count towards game. See BELOW THE LINE

ACCORDING TO HOYLE
Correct legally, ethically and according to custom. See HOYLE

ACE FROM ACE KING
Partnerships need to agree which card is to be led from suits headed by A K. The lead of the Ace from this combination is most common nowadays.

ACE LEAD
If a partnership's standard lead from A K against no trumps is the King, then the lead of the Ace is often conventionally a request for partner to play his highest card in the suit. See STRONG KINGS AND TENS

ACE SHOWING RESPONSES
A system of responses to forcing opening bids based on the assumption that opener is more interested in partner's first round controls than in general strength. It is most commonly played in conjunction with a conventional 2♣ opening bid. The responses are:

2♦	Negative (no Ace) and 5 or less points
2♡, 2♠, 3♣ or 3♦	Showing the Ace of the bid suit
2NT	Positive but Aceless
3NT	Showing two Aces
4NT	Showing three Aces

See CAB

ACES, THE
The name given to the American team of bridge professionals

formed by Ira Corn Jr. which won the World Championship in 1970, bringing the Bermuda Bowl back to North America for the first time in fifteen years. The team of Billy Eisenberg, Bobby Goldman, Bob Hamman, Jim Jacoby, Mike Lawrence and Bobby Wolff successfully defended the title in the following year. See WORLD CHAMPIONSHIPS

ACOL
A bidding system developed in the mid 1930s by Jack Marx and S J Simon. It takes its name from a venue in Acol Road in Hampstead where the two played and began to develop their theories. They were joined by Maurice Harrison-Gray and Iain Macleod and the then relatively unknown team enjoyed immediate tournament success, thereby popularizing the system. It has remained the most widespread system used in Britain.

ACOL 4NT OPENING BID
A specialized bid asking for Aces (not Blackwood). The responses are:

	Example
5♣ – no ace	
5◇ – ◇ A	♠ K Q J 10 8 6 5
5♡ – ♡ A	♡ A K Q J
5♠ – ♠ A	◇ –
5NT – 2 A	♣ A K
6♣ – ♣ A	

The merit of the Acol 4NT bid is shown by this example which can play in 6♠ in its own right. The Grand Slam depends only on discovering whether partner holds the ♠A. If the response to 4NT is 5♣ or 5◇, bid 6♠; if it is 5♠; bid 7♠, and over 5NT, bid 7NT.

ACOL LIGHT OPENER
An opening bid based on about 9 or 10 high-card points with a good six-card suit or two good five-card suits. See RULE OF NINETEEN

ACOL TWO BID
The use of an opening two-level bid in diamonds, hearts or spades as a one-round force to show a strong hand, normally with at least

eight playing tricks, which is not strong enough or unsuitable for a 2♣ opening. The bid promises either a six-card suit or two good five-carders. See FORCING TWO BID, STRONG TWO BID

ACTIVE DEFENCE
A positive attempt by the defenders to defeat a contract by taking or establishing tricks, usually involving the risk of losing tricks, as opposed to a passive defence where the emphasis is on not giving tricks away but waiting for the declarer to lose tricks.

ADJUSTED SCORE
A score assigned by the Director. If the Director judges that a pair or a team has suffered because of a transgression of the laws or ethics by opponents (even though the transgression is inadvertent), he is empowered to adjust the actual score recorded to establish an equitable result. If that is not possible he will allocate an artificial score. In a pairs event this will normally be 60% of the available matchpoints to the non-offending side and 40% to the offending side, or 50% to a side partly at fault.

ADVANCE CUE BID
A cue bid made when there is no apparent suit agreement. For example in the auction 1NT–NB–3♠–NB–4◊, the 4◊ bid is an advance cue bid. Opener's normal rebid would be either 3NT or 4♠, but here he is making a cue bid to imply that he has a good spade fit, maximum values for his 1NT opening and that he holds the ◊A. He is implicitly denying the ♣A by his failure to bid 4♣. With this information available, further action is up to his partner.

ADVANCE SACRIFICE
A sacrifice bid made before the opponents have reached their presumed contract.

AGGREGATE SCORE
Sum of all the scores obtained without conversion to IMPs. See INTERNATIONAL MATCH POINTS (IMPs)

ALCATRAZ COUP
An illegal play which, as the name suggests, should attract a severe penalty. The following is an example:

♠ A J 9

```
      N
  W       E
      S
```

♠ K 10 2

South, declarer, has to make three tricks in spades. Calling for the ♠J from dummy and receiving a small card from his right-hand opponent, he fails to follow suit. Fourth hand then either follows with the ♠Q or plays low. If low, declarer quickly corrects his revoke by substituting the ♠10. If the ♠Q is played, declarer corrects his revoke by producing the ♠K. His left-hand opponent can now change his card but South takes the marked finesse on the next round. See COFFEE-HOUSING

ALERT
Sponsoring organizations often require that a conventional bid be 'alerted' so that opponents become aware that it is not natural. Various ways of alerting may be specified but a common one is for the partner of the player making the conventional bid to tap on the table.

ALTERNATIVE SQUEEZE
A double squeeze position set up when the double squeeze may, or may not be 'on', but which will operate as a simple squeeze. For example:

♠ A   ♠ –
♡ 63   ♡ AKQ4
◇ 4   ◇ K
♣ K   ♣ –

```
      N
  W       E
      S
```

West playing in NTs. Only one opponent can hold four hearts. If this is South, and he also holds ♣A, he is squeezed when ♠A is played. If North guards the hearts, together with either ◇A or ♣A, he is squeezed by the play of ♠A. Dummy's ◊K is discarded, unless North discards ◊A.

AMBER
1 One of the traffic-light terms used by the Laws and Ethics Committee of the English Bridge Union to categorize psychic bids. An 'amber' psyche is one where the partnership's subsequent actions provide some evidence of an unauthorized partnership understanding but insufficient of themselves to warrant an adjusted score. See GREEN, PSYCHIC BID, RED
2 Shorthand for describing the vulnerability of both partnerships on a board, and meaning that both partnerships are vulnerable. See GREEN, RED, WHITE

ANALYSIS
The study of a hand to find the best possible line of play by declarer or defence.

ANCHOR SUIT
When some form of two-suited hand is shown, one of which is specified, the specified suit is called an anchor suit. See ASTRO, ASPTRO

APPEAL
A request for a review of a Tournament Director's ruling. In important events there is a procedure for requesting such a review by an Appeals Committee.

APPENDIX TABLE(S)
A useful adaptation of a Howell Movement (occasionally a Mitchell Movement) in order to accommodate extra tables without adding to the number of boards in play.

APPROACH FORCING
The basic principle behind most modern bidding systems, whereby a change of suit by an unpassed hand is treated as forcing for one round.

ARRANGEMENT OF TRICKS
At rubber bridge, one member of each partnership collects the cards played to each trick and arranges the tricks in front of him. At duplicate bridge, each player retains his cards arranging them face down in front of him, vertically if his side won the trick and horizontally otherwise.

ARRANGING
A one-word statement which may be made either when a player is still sorting his cards when it is his turn to bid, or by declarer when he wants to touch a card in dummy but does not wish to play it.

ARROW-SWITCH
The switching of North-South and East-West hands, usually on the last round or rounds of a Mitchell Movement, to provide a fairer comparison of scores across the field and produce a single winner. When an 'arrow-switch' is employed, the movement is called a Scrambled Mitchell. See MITCHELL, SCRAMBLED MITCHELL

ARTIFICIAL BID
A call which carries an unnatural meaning, for example Stayman, when a 2♣ bid says nothing about the bidder's club holding.

ASCENDING ORDER
The practice of making the cheapest bid, when responding or rebidding with two or three 4-card suits. This principle is employed in many bidding styles, with reservations about the quality of biddable suits.

ASKING BID
An 'asking bid' is a bid made by the member of a partnership wishing to take control of the auction which requests partner to give information about his hand, but does not itself directly convey any. Blackwood is the most commonly used asking bid.

ASPRO CONVENTION
A variation of ASTRO devised by Terence Reese (the name is

borrowed from a popular British brand of aspirin). After an opponent opens 1NT, 2♣ shows hearts and another suit and 2◇ shows spades and a minor suit. See DEFENCE TO 1NT

ASPTRO CONVENTION
A defence to a 1NT opening which, as the name implies, takes an element from both ASPRO and ASTRO. 2♣ shows hearts and another suit and 2◇ shows spades and another suit. The method has the advantage that two bids are used to show both major suits instead of one, thus improving definition. When holding both majors some partnerships prefer to treat their longer suit as the anchor suit, others use the shorter. See DEFENCE TO 1NT

ASSUMPTION
When a contract depends on the position of two or three key cards, it helps to make a definite 'assumption' about one of them. Plan of the play is then made, 'assuming' the key card is either badly- or well-placed, as the case may be.

ASTRO CONVENTION
This is a conventional defence to a 1NT opening whereby minor suit overcalls show two suits with at least nine cards between them. It derives its name from its inventors, Messrs. **A**llinger, **ST**ern and **RO**sler. 2♣ shows hearts and a minor and 2◇ shows spades and another suit. The major suit specified is called the anchor suit. See DEFENCE TO 1NT

ATTACKING LEAD
A lead which positively attempts to establish tricks for the defence as opposed to a passive lead which is simply intended to give no advantage to declarer. See PASSIVE LEAD

ATTITUDE SIGNALS
Signals made by a defender to encourage a continuation of the suit led, or to suggest a switch. Traditionally this is done by playing a high card to encourage and a low card to discourage.

AUCTION
The complete bidding sequence is known as 'the auction'.

AUCTION BRIDGE
The predecessor of modern Contract Bridge, Auction Bridge was first played in 1903 and the first code governing its play set up in 1908 by a joint committee of The Bath Club and The Portland Club. It gained rapid support and became more popular than similar games of the time (Bridge Whist for example) but was quickly superseded in 1926 by Contract Bridge.

AUTOBRIDGE
A commercial device, developed in America, with which pre-dealt hands can be used for self-teaching bidding and play.

AUTOMATIC SQUEEZE
A squeeze which works automatically against either opponent. For example:

♠ A K Q 3
♡ 4

♠ 4 2
♡ K 2
◇ A

When South leads the ◇A, discarding ♡4 from dummy, either opponent will be squeezed, if he holds four spades as well as the ♡A.

AVERAGE
Half the maximum number of matchpoints available on a hand at duplicate pairs. When, through its own fault, a pair is unable to play a board, the tournament director will usually award an average minus (40% of the total matchpoints available) and an average plus (60% of the total) to an innocent pair unable to play a board.

AVOIDANCE PLAY

A play designed to prevent a particular opponent gaining the lead. For example:

```
            A K 3 2
          ┌─────────┐
          │    N    │
  Q 8 7   │  W   E  │   J 10 9
          │    S    │
          └─────────┘
            6 5 4
```

If South, declarer, wishes to take three tricks in the suit without allowing East to gain the lead, he must start by leading a small card from hand. West plays low and dummy's King wins. South now re-enters his hand and leads a second card. Again West plays low and dummy's Ace wins. The third round can then safely be lost to West. If at any stage West contributes the Queen, South simply allows him to hold the trick.

BACKWARD FINESSE

A normal finesse is the lead of a card towards a tenace position, with the intention of playing the lower of the top two cards if the missing card is not forthcoming. However if the missing card is known to be over the tenace the finesse may be taken 'backwards'. For example:

```
            A 7 2
          ┌─────────┐
          │    N    │
          │  W   E  │
          │    S    │
          └─────────┘
            K J 9
```

Needing three tricks in the suit, South would normally play a small card from dummy towards the K J, playing East for the Queen. However, if South judges that West holds the Queen, he may play the Jack from hand. If West covers with the Queen,

North's Ace wins and a small card is played towards the K 9 finessing East for the 10.

BAD CARDS
1 Cards that are expected to prove valueless in the play of a hand.
2 A player who has been dealt consistently weak hands during a session of rubber bridge is said to have had 'bad cards'.

BALANCE OF STRENGTH
A partnership is said to possess the balance of strength when it has more high card points than their opponents.

BALANCED DISTRIBUTION
Hand distributions of 4–3–3–3, 4–4–3–2 and 5–3–3–2 (the first of these being described as 'completely balanced'). Hands of 5–4–2–2 or 6–3–2–2 distribution are sometimes described as 'semi-balanced'. An opening bid of 1NT usually shows a balanced hand, often with the further constraint that no five card major is held.

BALANCING
When a player is in the position such that to pass would end the bidding, he is said to be in the balancing position. For instance after the auction 1♣–NB–NB, the fourth player is in the balancing position. Since partner may have a fair hand, but no suitable overcall, it is often advisable for the player in that position to bid or to double for take out, even on slender values. See TAKE OUT DOUBLE

BAROMETER SCORING
The calculation and display of results round by round, rather than at the end of each session. This method is used especially at events where spectators are in attendance. The progress of the competitors is displayed on a leader-board in or near the playing area.

BARON SYSTEM
Leo Baron invented this system in the 1940s with the help of Adam Meredith. Several of their ideas have been incorporated in other systems, especially in modern Acol.

BARON OVER 2NT

In response to an opening bid of 2NT, a bid of 3♣ asks opener to show his lowest-ranking four-card or longer suit. The partners may continue to show four-card suits in ascending order up to the level of 3NT.

BARON SLAM TRY

A convention whereby a bid in the suit below the agreed trump suit at the five- or six-level asks partner to bid a slam (small or grand) if his trump holding is better than could be expected from his previous bidding.

BARON TWO NO TRUMP RESPONSE

Stemming directly from the work of Leo Baron, the 2NT response to an opening suit bid at the one-level is game forcing, showing 16–18 points and a balanced distribution, although modern practice is for simply 16+ points and a balanced distribution. Both opener and responder are expected to bid four-card (or longer) suits upwards until a suitable fit has been located, or 3NT reached.

BARRAGE

Another term for pre-emptive bidding.

BATH COUP

A hold-up after a King (from K Q) lead towards an A-J combination which forces the leader to switch or concede a trick to both the Ace and Jack. For example:

```
              762
               N
  KQ1098   W      E   43
               S
              AJ5
```

West leads the King on which South plays the 5.

BATTLE OF THE CENTURY

In the winter of 1931, Ely Culbertson challenged Sidney Lenz to a match over 150 rubbers, Lenz playing the then 'official' system, and Culbertson his own. The match (dubbed 'The Battle of the Century') was won by Culbertson by 8980 points and resulted in the wide acceptance of Culbertson's ideas on bidding.

BED
A player is said to have 'gone to bed with an Ace' if, having had the opportunity to cash it earlier, he fails to take it at all.

BELONG
A hand is said to 'belong' to a side if they can make the optimum contract.

BELOW THE LINE
Phrase used in rubber bridge to identify scores entered below the horizontal line on the score sheet. Only scores counting towards game are so entered. See ABOVE THE LINE

BENJAMINISED ACOL (BENJAMIN CONVENTION)
Benjaminised Acol (Benji-Acol), devised by Albert Benjamin from Scotland, is Acol with a revised system of two-level openings to allow an Acol player the opportunity to use two-bids in the majors as weak. 2◇ (with a negative 2♡ response) is used to show a hand which would be opened 2♣ in traditional ACOL and 2♣ (negative 2◇) is used to show an eight-playing trick hand in an unspecified suit. Note that many players use an opening 2NT to show a balanced 19–20 points and the sequence 2♣–NB–2◇–NB–2NT to show a balanced hand with 21–22 points. Some players interchange the 2♣ and 2◇ openings (Reverse Benjaminised Acol).

BERMUDA BOWL
See WORLD CHAMPIONSHIPS

BETTER MINOR
In some systems, such as five-card major systems, it is necessary to open in a minor suit with fewer than four cards. Playing the 'better minor' method a minor-suit opening always guarantees at least

three cards. With a three-card holding in both minors some partnerships always open 1♣, others choose the better quality suit, but both styles are referred to as 'better minor'.

BID
Any call which includes the naming of a denomination and thereby undertakes to win a certain number of tricks in that denomination. See CALLS

BIDDABLE SUIT
A suit which complies with minimum requirements in terms of length and strength for it to be bid. A holding such as Q J x x used to be regarded as the minimum for a four-card suit, whilst all five-card suits were considered biddable. In the modern style any suit of four cards is considered biddable.

BIDDING BOXES
Swedish invention permitting silent bidding. Each player, instead of vocally making his bid, takes a card from a complete set of indexed cards held in a small holder and places it in front of him on the table.

BIDDING CHALLENGE
Feature of some bridge magazines whereby readers are given a number of pairs of hands to bid, comparing their bidding with that of a panel of experts.

BIDDING SPACE
The space available for making bids. The cheaper the bid, the less bidding space is used up. For example the 1◇ bid in the auction 1♣–NB–1◇ uses minimal bidding space, but 1◇–NB–2♣ uses up significantly more. In constructive bidding, it is usually preferable to conserve bidding space (at least until a fit is found) in order to exchange the maximum amount of information. Conversely it is often in the interest of the defenders to restrict the amount of space available to the opposition, for instance by making pre-emptive bids.

BIDDING SYSTEM

The sum total of partnership understandings and conventions which form the language of the bidding. See INFERENCE BID

BIT

Slang term for a small card as in 'Ace-bit' (A x).

BLACK POINTS

See LOCAL POINTS

BLACKWOOD CONVENTION

In its most basic form, a bid of 4NT when a trump suit has been agreed asks partner to show how many Aces he holds. In response:

    5♣ Shows zero or four Aces
    5◇ Shows one Ace
    5♡ Shows two Aces
    5♠ Shows three Aces

After the response to Blackwood, 5NT may be used to ask for Kings on a similar scale but with 6NT, not 6♣, showing four Kings. See also: BYZANTINE, FIVE ACE, ROMAN, ROMAN KEY CARD

BLANKET LICENCE (GENERAL AND RESTRICTED)

Term used by the Laws and Ethics Committee of the English Bridge Union to denote that certain treatments or developments in the bidding are authorized.

BLOCK

A suit is said to be blocked if it is impossible, without the use of an outside entry, to play out the suit by cashing top cards. For example:

A

```
    N
  W   E
    S
```

KQJ3

In order that the above suit may be cashed, South must possess an outside entry since the Ace will win the first trick in the North hand.

BLOCKBUSTER
A very powerful hand.

BLOCKING PLAY
A play made in an attempt to cause a block in the opponents' suit. For example:

```
                 A 2
              ┌───────┐
              │   N   │
     K J 7 6 3│ W   E │ Q 5
              │   S   │
              └───────┘
               10 9 8 4
```

West leads the 6 against South's no trump contract. The play of the Ace from dummy will block the suit. East cannot play the Queen without conceding a trick and similarly, when East is on lead and returns the Queen, West is unable to overtake without conceding a trick.

BLUE CLUB SYSTEM
System used by the Italian Blue Team during their long string of World Championship victories. Developed mainly by Benito Garozzo and Leon Yallouze, the system is based on an artificial 1♣ opening (17+ points) and canape. See CANAPE

BLUE CLUB RESPONSES
A method of responding to a 2NT enquiry following a weak-two opener in a major. The 'Blue Club Responses' are:

    3♣   Minimum opener; poor quality suit
    3◊   Minimum opener; good quality suit
    3♡   Maximum opener; poor quality suit
    3♠   Maximum opener; good quality suit
  3 NT Solid suit headed by AKQ

BLUE TEAM

The name given to the enormously successful international Italian team, so-called after their triumph over the Red team in the 1956 Italian trials. From 1957 until 1975 the Blue Team won every Bermuda Bowl World Championship it contested (it did not participate in 1970/71) and the 1964, 1968 and 1972 Olympiads. The three best-known players in this period were Giorgio Belladonna, Pietro Forquet and Benito Garozzo. The team divided into two schools of thought over bidding, which led to the development of the Neapolitan Club (forerunner of the Blue Club) and the Roman Club. See WORLD CHAMPIONSHIPS

BOARD

1 A device used in duplicate bridge (showing the hand number, dealer, vulnerability and compass points) with four slots to house the hands and another for the travelling scoreslip. Plastic or leather wallets are also used for the same purpose.
2 The table on which the cards are played.
3 The dummy's hand (due to its lying on the table).

BODY

That part of the hand excluding the honour cards. The quality of the body can significantly influence the value of the hand, particularly in judging whether to bid marginal games.

BONUS

Different bonuses are awarded in all types of bridge.

In **Rubber Bridge** the bonuses are:

Vulnerable Grand Slam	1500
Non-vulnerable Grand Slam	1000
Vulnerable Small Slam	750
Non-vulnerable Small Slam	500
Rubber completed in two games	700
Rubber completed in three games	500
One game in an incomplete rubber	300
Partscore in an incomplete rubber	100
Successful doubled contract	50

Successful redoubled contract	100
Five trump honours in one hand	150
Four trump honours in one hand	100
Four Aces in one hand at no trumps	150

In **Chicago Bridge** the bonuses are:

Vulnerable Grand Slam	1500
Non-vulnerable Grand Slam	1000
Vulnerable Small Slam	750
Non-vulnerable Small Slam	500
Vulnerable game	500
Non-vulnerable game	300
Partscore bid and made on last hand	100
Successful doubled contract	50
Successful redoubled contract	100
Five trump honours in one hand	150
Four trump honours in one hand	100
Four Aces in one hand at no trumps	150

In **Duplicate Bridge** the bonuses are:

Vulnerable Grand Slam	1500
Non-vulnerable Grand Slam	1000
Vulnerable Small Slam	750
Non-vulnerable Small Slam	500
Vulnerable game	500
Non-vulnerable game	300
Partscore	50
Successful doubled contract	50
Successful redoubled contract	100

BOOK
The first six tricks won by the declaring side. The term originates from the practice by declarer of placing the first six tricks won in a single pile, a 'book'.

BOTTOM
A score of zero matchpoints on a board in a duplicate event.

BOXED
A hand or deck of cards is said to be 'boxed' if one or more of the cards is faced.

BREAK
1 The distribution of the outstanding cards in a suit between the unseen hands. Also used to describe a perfectly even break (e.g. 3–3), or a nearly even break when an odd number of cards is missing (e.g. 3–2). For example: 'If the clubs break...'
2 To defeat a contract.

BRIDGE
A partnership game derived from Whist. The term is used to refer to three games; Bridge Whist, Auction Bridge and Contract Bridge. The first recorded mention of a game like Bridge was in 1886 when a pamphlet was published about the game Biritch or Russian Whist. There is little evidence to suggest that the game did originate in Russia, although it does bear a close resemblance to Vint which is a game of Russian origin. The name Bridge is simply a corruption of 'Biritch'. Due to the dominance of Contract Bridge, the term is nowadays considered synonymous with Contract Bridge. There are several variations of Contract Bridge including Rubber Bridge, Chicago Bridge (four deal bridge) and Duplicate Bridge (Pairs, Teams or Individuals).

BRIDGERAMA
Method of displaying bridge to an audience. First used in the 1958 World Championship but, due to the requirement for a great number of operators, it has been replaced by VuGraph since the 1970s. See VUGRAPH

BRING IN
To 'bring in' a suit for three tricks means to make three tricks in that suit.

BRITISH BRIDGE LEAGUE
Body responsible for representing Britain in international bridge matters including the selection of British teams. Formed by Alfred

Manning-Foster in 1931, its constituents are the English Bridge Union, the Scottish Bridge Union, the Welsh Bridge Union and the Northern Ireland Bridge Union.

BROKEN SEQUENCE
A sequence of honour cards (but including the 9) with one of the middle cards missing, for example K J 10 9, A Q J, A K J 10.

BUENOS AIRES AFFAIR
This refers to the 1965 Bermuda Bowl World Championship when the British pair, Terence Reese and Boris Schapiro, was accused of cheating by transmitting information regarding the length of their heart suits with finger signals. Although at the time the World Bridge Federation executive committee found Reese and Schapiro guilty, a subsequent independent enquiry headed by Sir John Foster QC and General Lord Bourne found, after ten months consideration, that the charges were unfounded. Arguments for both sides may be found in the books *The Story of an Accusation* by Terence Reese and *The Great Bridge Scandal* by Alan Truscott.

BUSINESS DOUBLE
See PENALTY DOUBLE

BUST
A seemingly useless hand.

BUSY CARD
A card which has some definite purpose in the play of a hand, as opposed to an idle card which may be safely discarded. The term usually refers to an important card in a squeeze position.

BUTCHER
Slang term meaning to misplay, especially to misplay very badly. 'Carve' and 'Misère' are similar terms.

BUTLER METHOD
A method of scoring duplicate pairs events in terms of IMPs. The scores for each board are averaged to produce a datum score (in a

large field the top and bottom scores are ignored). Each pair's score is then calculated relative to the datum and converted to IMPs. See INTERNATIONAL MATCH POINTS (IMPs)

BUY
In a competitive auction a player is said to have bought the contract if the opponents do not compete further.

BYE-LAWS
Rules determined by the the national bridge organisations governing their membership.

BYZANTINE BLACKWOOD
A sophisticated version of Blackwood, based on the concept of Key cards and Half-Key cards in the suits bid by the partnership. Each response to the 4NT enquiry can have several meanings:

5♣	no ace ·	5♦	A	5♡	A A
	A A A		A A A A		A K Q
	A A K		A A A K		A K K
					A K k

5♠	A A KQ	5NT	A A A KQ	A – Ace
	A K KQ		A A K KQ	K – Key King
	A A K K		A A A K K	KQ – Key King-Queen
	A A A k		A KQ KQ	k – Half-Key King

A Key suit is one which has been both bid and supported by the partnership. A Half-Key suit is one introduced by the 4NT bidder but not supported or, if no such suit exists, one bid by responder to the 4NT bidder but not supported.

A bid of 5NT after 4NT confirms possession of all the Aces and asks partner how many additional features he holds. Any unshown King or any Key-Suit Queen counts as one feature; any unshown King-Queen counts as two features. Responses are on the basic step principle:

    6♣ no feature
    6♦ one feature
    6♡ two features etc

—C—

CAB
Natural system of bidding not dissimilar to Acol, particular features of which are Ace-showing responses to the 2♣ opener and Blackwood. CAB stands for two **C**lubs, **A**ce responses and **B**lackwood. See ACE SHOWING RESPONSES, BLACKWOOD, TWO CLUB SYSTEMS

CADDY
An assistant who collects score cards at a large tournament.

CALCUTTA
A duplicate tournament making possible a fair-sized financial gain to any player or other participant. After the entries have been made, an auction is held at which players and spectators bid to place bets on contesting pairs. The money bet is put into a pool and distributed among the purchasers of the winning pair.

CALL
Any bid, double, redouble or pass.

CAMROSE TROPHY
Annual tournament contested by England, Wales, Scotland and Northern Ireland (and formerly Eire) under the auspices of the British Bridge League.

CANAPE
A bidding style in which, with two suits, the shorter suit is bid first. The style was originally developed by Pierre Albarran in France and has influenced Italian bidding theory. It was incorporated in the Neapolitan Club, Blue Club and Roman systems.

CANSINO CONVENTION
Defence to a 1NT opening bid where an overcall of 2♣ shows clubs and two other suits, and a 2◊ overcall shows both majors. See DEFENCE TO 1NT

CAPTAINCY

1 When one member of a partnership has made a limit bid, the other takes the 'captaincy' and selects the contract.
2 The captain of a team. His responsibilities include scoring, selecting line-ups, arranging the match venue (for private matches) etc.

CARD READING

The determination of the distribution of the unseen hands and the location of the missing high cards by logical deduction from the bidding and play.

CARRY-OVER SCORE

When a tournament is played over more than one session, the 'carry-over' score is that part of the score carried over from a previous session.

CARVE

Slang term meaning to misplay. 'Butcher' and 'Misère' are similar terms.

CASH

To lead a winning card or cards.

CASH OUT

To take a series of tricks by leading winning cards. The term is usually applied to the situation when a player realizes that he is on lead for the last time and takes all the tricks that he can.

CHANGE OF SUIT

The bid of a different suit.

CHEAPEST BID

The most economical bid available to a player.

CHEST ONE'S CARDS

To hold one's cards tight to one's chest to prevent the opponents from seeing them.

CHICAGO

A form of rubber bridge whereby each rubber comprises exactly four hands with pre-determined vulnerability. On the first deal neither side is vulnerable and on the fourth both sides are. On the other two deals, by prior agreement, one side is vulnerable. Scoring is similar to rubber bridge but with bonuses for games replacing the rubber bonus. If a hand is passed out it is redealt by the same player.

CHICANE

Another expression for Void.

CHINESE FINESSE

A deceptive play intended to make an opponent think an honour lead is the higher of a sequence of honours. For example:

a)

```
              A 4 3
            ┌───────┐
            │   N   │
K 8 6 2     │ W   E │   J 10 7
            │   S   │
            └───────┘
              Q 9 5
```

b)

```
              A 4 3
            ┌───────┐
            │   N   │
K 8 6 2     │ W   E │   10 7 5
            │   S   │
            └───────┘
              Q J 9
```

If South, as declarer with hand a), judges that West holds the King he may lead the Queen (suggesting he holds the Jack) hoping it will not be covered. On hand b), West would be right not to cover since South could then finesse holding J 9 over 10 7.

CHUKKER

A term for the four deals at Chicago bridge. The term is borrowed from polo. See CHICAGO

CLAIM

Declarer makes a claim by placing his cards face up on the table and announcing that he will win one or more of the remaining tricks. Defender makes a claim by showing any or all of his cards to declarer and announcing he will win one or more of the remaining tricks. When a player makes a claim he should state his intended line of play. If he fails to do so and the claim is contested then a restriction on his play may be imposed. In duplicate, when there is a Director present, if a claim is disputed play ceases and the Director must be called to adjudicate.

CLEAR A SUIT
To force out by successive leads adversely held high cards and so establish winners in the suit.

CLOSED HAND
The hand of the declarer as distinct from the 'open' hand, the dummy.

CLOSED ROOM
In head-to-head teams-of-four matches, the two pairs of a team usually play in different rooms. One of these rooms may be designated the 'closed room', the other the 'open room'. Spectators may watch in the open room but may not enter the closed room.

COFFEE-HOUSING
Indulging in unethical behaviour in an attempt to mislead the opponents. For example:

```
            K J
          ┌─────┐
          │  N  │
      Q 2 │ W E │ A 3
          │  S  │
          └─────┘
            5 4
```

On the lead of a small card from South, who is playing the contract, West pauses for thought before playing low, as he would if he held the Ace instead of the Queen, thus misleading declarer. The term originates from a style of bridge that used to be played in European coffee houses.

COLD
Slang term describing a contract which is certain to make. 'Frigid' and 'Icy' are similar terms.

COME-ON SIGNAL
A signal which encourages partner to continue playing a suit. See ATTITUDE

COMMUNICATIONS
The ability to transfer the lead between the two hands of a partnership.

COMPASS POINTS
North–South–East–West indicate the positions of players at the table.

COMPETITIVE AUCTION
Bidding sequences in which both partnerships enter the auction.

COMPETITIVE DOUBLE
A double, primarily for take out, but conveying the message that the bidder is unwilling to pass but has no satisfactory descriptive bid to make.

COMPOUND SQUEEZE
A preparatory triple squeeze, followed by a double squeeze. The ending requires two double menaces (guarded by both opponents) and a one-card menace. The one-card menace must be positioned over the opponent to be threatened, and declarer has all the remaining tricks but one.

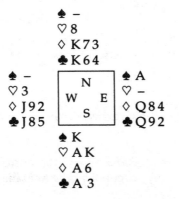

In No Trumps, South leads ♡A and East is squeezed in three suits. He must discard from one of his minor suits. South next plays the King and Ace of whichever minor suit East discards, and then leads the ♡K, which creates a double squeeze on both opponents.

COMPUTER DEAL
Term to describe the dealing of hands by computer. These hands are commonly more distributional than hands dealt by the players. This is because players often do not shuffle the cards properly.

CONCEDE
To give one or more tricks to the opposition.

CONCESSION
A player makes a concession when he announces he will lose the remaining tricks or agrees to a claim by the opposition.

CONDONE
To bid or play immediately following an irregularity and thereby convert it into a legal action.

CONGRESS
A tournament, typically played over a (long) weekend, and often comprising several individual competitions.

CONSOLATION EVENT
In most congresses and large tournaments, the main event has qualifying rounds to reach the Final. A 'consolation event' is usually run concurrently with the Final for the pairs/teams which failed to qualify.

CONSTRUCTIVE
Description of a bid which is helpful and forward-going.

CONTRACT
The undertaking by declarer to win the number of tricks, in the denomination named, specified by the final bid of the auction.

CONTRACT BRIDGE

Contract Bridge evolved slowly from the game of Whist, through the games of Auction Whist, Auction Bridge and finally to Contract Bridge in 1926. It differed from its predecessors in that only tricks bid for and made counted towards game (based on the Plafond system). The method of scoring was changed considerably by Harold Vanderbilt who perfected the new game with the inclusion of incentives for games and slams, as well as the Plafond system of bidding towards game by accumulating partscores.

CONTROL

A holding in a suit that prevents opponents from cashing more than a certain number of tricks in the suit. An Ace or void (in a suit contract) constitutes a first round control, a King or singleton (in a suit contract) constitutes a second round control. In some systems, notably the Blue Club, Aces and Kings are given numerical values: Aces two, Kings one. Responses to the strong 1♣ opening show how many controls are held.

CONTROLLED PSYCHES

A psychic bid is one which deliberately violates a partnership agreement. A psychic bid which can be controlled by some special bid by partner is called a controlled psyche and makes the use of such bids safer. British licensing restrictions prohibit the use of controlled psyches. See PSYCHIC BID

CONVENTION

A call or play with a defined meaning understood by the partnership which has little or no similarity to the natural use of the bid. See ALERT

CONVENTION CARD

A card on which both members of a partnership give details of the system of bidding they are using and their methods of leads, discards and signals. It varies from the simple, acceptable in most local clubs, to the very detailed information which is required by sponsoring organisations for major tournaments.

CO-OPERATIVE DOUBLE

A double, usually at a low level, which shows a willingness either to bid on or to penalise the opponents but with no strong preference between the two. See COMPETITIVE DOUBLE

COUNT SIGNALS

A signal to convey information about the length of a suit rather than its strength. In standard methods a peter (high-low) shows an even number of cards.

COUNT SQUEEZE

A method of squeezing a player who does not guard a crucial suit, in order to drop a singleton honour, instead of taking a losing finesse. Declarer has a count of the hand and knows that West holds ♠A in this example.

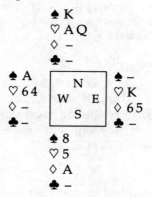

South leads ◊A and West must discard a heart and dummy discards ♠K. When a heart is next led and West follows low, declarer will drop East's singleton King, because he knows that West's last card is ♠A.

COUNTING ONE'S CARDS

The Laws of Duplicate Contract Bridge state that each player should count his cards, before he looks at his hand, to check that he has thirteen.

COUNTING THE HAND
The deduction of the location of the cards in the unseen hands from the bidding and previous play.

COUP
A specialized manoeuvre during the play of the hand. Many coups are given identifying names, some descriptive, others from the names of their authors or the places where they first surfaced. See ALCATRAZ, BATH, EN PASSANT, CROCODILE, DESCHAPELLES, DEVIL'S, GRAND, MERRIMAC, MORTON'S FORK, SCISSORS, TRUMP, VIENNA

COUP EN PASSANT
The lead of a plain suit card to promote a low trump sitting over a high trump. For example:

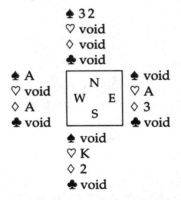

```
              ♠ 3 2
              ♡ void
              ◇ void
              ♣ void
♠ A        ┌─────────┐        ♠ void
♡ void     │    N    │        ♡ A
◇ A        │ W     E │        ◇ 3
♣ void     │    S    │        ♣ void
           └─────────┘
              ♠ void
              ♡ K
              ◇ 2
              ♣ void
```

In the diagram above, with hearts as trumps, a spade is led from the North hand. If East discards, South ruffs and, if East ruffs, South's King is promoted as a winner.

COURT CARDS
Old-fashioned name for the Honours. Originating from the fact that the Kings, Queens and Jacks, being all 'coated' figures were known as 'coat cards'. This was quickly corrupted to 'court cards' due to the association with a royal court.

COURTESY BID
A response made on a very weak hand to allow for the possibility that the opener has great strength.

COVERING HONOURS
The maxim 'Cover an honour with an honour' coming from the early days of whist is usually sound bridge technique but may sometimes be wrong. See CHINESE FINESSE

CRASHING HONOURS
The playing of two high honours by defenders to the same trick. A deceptive play by declarer can sometimes induce defenders to crash their honours. For example:

```
            Q5432
          ┌───────┐
          │   N   │
      A   │ W   E │  K6
          │   S   │
          └───────┘
           J10987
```

If South, declarer, leads the Queen from dummy, East may decide to cover, causing the defenders to crash their honours.

CRISP VALUES
Aces and Kings.

CRISS-CROSS SQUEEZE
A squeeze with a blocked suit. For example:

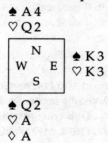

```
            ♠ A4
            ♡ Q2
          ┌───────┐
          │   N   │   ♠ K3
          │ W   E │   ♡ K3
          │   S   │
          └───────┘
            ♠ Q2
            ♡ A
            ◊ A
```

South leads the ◊A and discards the ♠4 from dummy. Both the hearts and spades are now blocked but South can unblock whichever suit East discards and use the other suit as an entry to the then established queen. See SQUEEZE

CROCKFORDS CLUB
The gaming house in central London which became famous for its high-stake games in the early days of rubber bridge, and the prominent players who supported it. The club is now a casino and bridge is no longer played regularly.

CROCODILE COUP
A play by a defender of an apparently unnecessarily high card to prevent his partner from being thrown in. The defender can be imagined as a crocodile opening its jaws in order to make certain that it catches partner's winning card (which by this stage is a singleton). For example:

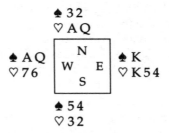

```
                    ♠ 3 2
                    ♡ A Q
                    ┌─────────┐
     ♠ A Q          │    N    │      ♠ K
     ♡ 7 6          │  W   E  │      ♡ K 5 4
                    │    S    │
                    └─────────┘
                    ♠ 5 4
                    ♡ 3 2
```

If South, declarer, leads a spade West must play his ♠A, swallowing his partner's ♠K, in order to prevent East from winning and having to lead into the heart tenace.

CROSS-IMP
A method of scoring a pairs competition in terms of IMPs. Each pair's score is compared with the score of every other pair sitting in the opposite direction and converted to IMPs. as if the other pair were team-mates. A pair's score on any given board is then the sum (plus or minus) of all the separate IMP scores. See BUTLER METHOD, INTERNATIONAL MATCH POINTS (IMPs)

CROSSRUFF

A play in which trumps in both hands are used to ruff losers rather than draw trumps. It is usually correct to play off side suit winners before starting to crossruff in order to prevent opponents discarding those suits and later being in a position to ruff declarer's winners.

CROWHURST CONVENTION

A convention, named after the English player Eric Crowhurst, whereby a bid of 2♣ by responder, after a wide-range 1NT rebid by opener, is used as an enquiry. For example, if the 1NT rebid by opener shows 12–16 points then the continuations after the sequence:

Opener	Responder
1♡	1♠
1NT	2♣
?	

would be:

2◊ 12–14 points without five hearts or three spades
2♡ 12–14 points with five hearts
2♠ 12–14 points with three spades
2NT 15–16 points

CUE BID

Basically this is a bid of a suit with no intention that the bid suit should be considered as the trump suit. The term is used to cover several quite different situations. When the possibility of a slam is being investigated and the trump suit has been agreed (either explicitly or implicitly), then the cue bid of a suit shows a control in that suit. By partnership agreement this may be first round control (an Ace or void), or either first or second round control. (See ADVANCE CUE BID, SPLINTER BID). In a contested auction the cue bid of an opponent's suit may be used as a general forcing bid (when no suitable alternative is available) or to convey a specific message or request. (See DIRECTIONAL ASKING BID, UNASSUMING CUE BID). When an opponent's opening bid is directly overcalled in the same suit, the message conveyed is either a very powerful hand or, more popularly, some form of two-suited hand. (See GHESTEM, MICHAELS CUE BID)

CULBERTSON SYSTEM
System of bidding devised and popularized by Ely Culbertson, first published in the Blue Book in 1933 and later revised in further Blue Books. Many of the features of the Culbertson system have provided a basis for modern methods. The system was influenced by the very successful Four Aces team and by public opinion, leading to the publication of the Gold Book in 1936 which became standard in America for nearly fifteen years. Features of the system were:
1 Valuation by Honour Tricks,
2 Uniform standards for biddable suits,
3 The approach forcing principle,
4 The forcing Two bids,
5 The forcing take-out showing three Honour Tricks,
6 Strong No Trump,
7 Non-forcing jump rebids by opener, unless in a new suit,
8 Asking bids.

CULBERTSON 4–5NT
A slam convention showing Aces and Kings as well as asking for them. The 4NT bid shows three Aces or two Aces and a King of a suit bid by the partnership. The responses are: With two Aces or one Ace and a King of a suit bid by the partnership, bid 5NT. Holding no Ace, bid five of the lowest suit that has been bid by the partnership . Holding one Ace, bid the suit with the Ace at the five-level, or at the six-level if it is the Ace of the lowest suit genuinely bid by the partnership.

CURSE OF SCOTLAND
Name given to the ◊9. Various explanations have been suggested:
1 In the game Pope Joan, the ◊9 was called the Pope, the Antichrist of Scotland.
2 In the game Cornette, introduced to Scotland by the unfortunate Mary Queen of Scots, the ◊9 was the chief card.
3 'Butcher' Cumberland wrote the orders for the Battle of Culloden (1746) on the card.
4 The order for the massacre at Glencoe was signed on the back of the card.

5   That it is derived from the nine lozenges that formed the arms of the Earl of Star, who was hated for his part in the massacre at Glencoe and the union with England.

CURTAIN CARD
Written record of a hand in a duplicate board which enables a player to check that his hand is correct and which is also used to restore the hand if the board become fouled.

CUT
1   Before the beginning of a rubber, a deck of cards is spread face down on the table and each player draws one card. Those drawing the two highest cards partner each other.
2   Before every deal the deck is cut, towards the dealer, by dividing it into two portions. The lower portion is replaced on top of the other.
3   To ruff.
4   The place at which the field is divided in a qualifying session to decide who goes forward to the next stage.

CUT IN
In rubber bridge, the draw for partners. In a club, it distinguishes a session when members turn up and draw randomly for partners after each rubber, from one in which two players partner each other for the whole time.

CUT THROAT BRIDGE
A version of so-called three-handed bridge. See THREE-HANDED BRIDGE

—D—

DAB
An acronym for 'Directional Asking Bid'. See DIRECTIONAL ASKING BID

DANGER HAND

During the play of a contract, it can be dangerous to lose the lead to one opponent but safe to lose it to the other. The hand that declarer needs to prevent gaining the lead is termed the 'danger hand'. Sometimes declarer can organize life accordingly:

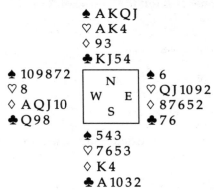

```
                    ♠ A K Q J
                    ♡ A K 4
                    ◇ 9 3
                    ♣ K J 5 4
     ♠ 109872      ┌─────────┐      ♠ 6
     ♡ 8           │    N    │      ♡ Q J 10 9 2
     ◇ A Q J 10    │ W     E │      ◇ 87652
     ♣ Q 9 8       │    S    │      ♣ 76
                   └─────────┘
                    ♠ 543
                    ♡ 7653
                    ◇ K 4
                    ♣ A 10 3 2
```

Playing in 3NT, South receives the lead of the ♠10. He has eight top tricks and can develop a ninth in clubs. He has a two-way finesse available in the suit. He should however finesse the 10 so that, if the finesse loses, West, the safe hand, is on lead. Should East gain the lead, a diamond switch could be fatal.

DATUM

The average score obtained on a board in an event with Butler scoring. In a large field, one or more of the top and bottom scores are ignored to give a more representative score. Each individual result is compared to the datum and converted to IMPs. See BUTLER METHOD, INTERNATIONAL MATCH POINTS (IMPs)

DEAD

A hand is said to be 'dead' if there is no entry to it.

DEAL

1 To distribute the 52 cards, one card to each player in turn starting with the player on the left of the dealer.
2 The set of four hands dealt.

DEALER
The person who deals and also makes the first call.

DECEPTIVE PLAY
The play of a card, or a line of play, with the express intention of deceiving opponents about the true lie of the cards.

DECK
A pack of playing cards.

DECLARATION
The final contract.

DECLARER
The player who first bid the denomination of the final contract.

DEEP FINESSE
A finesse when three or more cards higher than the card finessed are missing.

```
            A J 9
          ┌─────────┐
          │    N    │
          │  W   E  │
          │    S    │
          └─────────┘
            4 3 2
```

Needing two tricks in the above suit and with plenty of entries to hand, South plays a low card from hand planning to play the 9 if West follows with a low card. If the 9 loses to the King or Queen, South can later take a simple finesse of the Jack.

DEFEAT THE CONTRACT
To win, in defence, enough tricks so that declarer cannot make his contract even if he wins all the remaining tricks.

DEFECTIVE TRICK
A trick that contains fewer, or more than four legally played cards.

DEFENCE, THE
1 The two defenders.
2 The line of play adopted by the defenders.

DEFENCE TO 1NT
Term given to a partnership agreement about entering the bidding after an opponent's 1NT opening bid. See ASPRO, ASPTRO, ASTRO, CANSINO, LANDY, RIPSTRA, SHARPLES

DEFENCE TO ARTIFICIAL STRONG CLUB
Term given to a partnership agreement about entering the bidding after an opponent's strong artificial 1♣ opening bid. See TRUSCOTT

DEFENCE TO MULTI
Term given to partnership agreement about entering the bidding after an opponent's Multicoloured Two Diamond opener. Many variations exist, mostly based on methods originally put forward by the English player, Chris Dixon. See DIXON DEFENCE

DEFENCE TO OPENING THREE-BID
Term given to a partnership agreement about entering the bidding after an opponent's pre-emptive three-level opening. See FILM, FISHBEIN, FOXU, LMX, LOWER MINOR, OPTIONAL DOUBLE

DEFENDERS
1 During the auction, the non-opening side.
2 During the play, the non-declaring side.

DEFENSIVE BIDDING
Bidding by the non-opening side, sometimes with an obstructive intent.

DEFENSIVE TRICK
A card combination which wins a trick in defence.

DELAYED GAME RAISE
When partner opens one of a major suit and the responder has

values for game, it is valuable to distinguish between hands with distributional values, and hands with trump support and all round strength (usually 13 to 15 points). In the first case a direct raise to game, which has the additional value of having a preemptive effect, is in order. In the second case the nature of the hand is best described by bidding a second suit and then bidding game in partner's opening suit at the next opportunity – a delayed game raise.

DELAYED SUPPORT

An invitational raise in partner's first bid suit on the second round of bidding usually showing three-card support, as in the sequence: 1♡–NB–2♣–NB–2◊–NB–3♡.

DENIAL BID

A bid that indicates lack of support for partner's suit, or general weakness such as the 2◊ response to an Acol 2♣ opening. See HERBERT NEGATIVE, NEGATIVE RESPONSE

DENOMINATION

A general term meaning clubs, diamonds, hearts, spades, or No Trumps.

DEPO

Convention handling intervention after a Blackwood 4NT bid. The name is a mnemonic for 'Double Even Pass Odd'. A double after intervention shows zero, two or four Aces, the pass shows one or three.

DESCHAPELLES COUP

Defensive play involving the sacrifice of a high card in order to gain entry to partner's hand. For example:

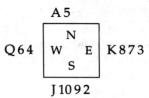

A 5

Q 6 4 | W   E | K 8 7 3

J 10 9 2

Requiring an entry into partner's hand, East makes the Deschapelles coup by leading the King. If South, the declarer, takes the King with dummy's Ace, the Queen is now an entry, and if declarer ducks the King, East simply leads another card establishing an extra trick.

DEUCE
A name often used in reference to the Two. Derivative from *deux* (French) and *duo* (Latin).

DEVIL'S COUP or COUP DU DIABLE
A coup whereby a seemingly certain trump loser vanishes. For example:

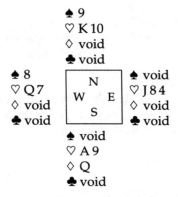

♠ 9
♥ K 10
♦ void
♣ void

♠ 8   ♠ void
♥ Q 7   ♥ J 8 4
♦ void   ♦ void
♣ void   ♣ void

♠ void
♥ A 9
♦ Q
♣ void

Hearts are trumps, and South, declarer, leads the ♠9 from dummy. East ruffs, and South overruffs. If East ruffs with the ♥J, South ruffs with the ♥A, and finesses the ♥10. If East trumps with a lower card, South ruffs with the ♥9 and takes the top two trumps for the final two tricks.

DIRECT KING CONVENTION
If during the auction a member of the partnership reveals how many Aces he has, a subsequent Blackwood 4NT enquiry will ask him about Kings. See BLACKWOOD, SWISS CONVENTION

DIRECTION
North, South, East or West.

DIRECTIONAL ASKING BID (DAB)
After an overcall, a cue bid of the opponent's suit by the opening side asks partner to bid No Trumps if he holds a partial stopper in the suit bid by the opposition.

DIRECTOR
See TOURNAMENT DIRECTOR

DISCARD
A card played to a trick which is not of the suit led and not the trump suit.

DISCOURAGING CARD
A card signalling the fact that a defender does not wish a suit to be continued or led. See ATTITUDE SIGNALS

DISCOVERY PLAY
A declarer who tests the distribution of the outstanding cards in the unseen hands before committing himself to one line of play is said to be making a 'discovery play'. For example:

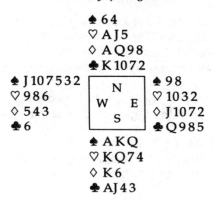

West leads ♠J against South's 7NT. Delclarer has twelve top tricks and the thirteenth will come from a successful finesse of ♣Q. By playing off all the top winners in spades, hearts and diamonds, declarer 'discovers' that West started with a 6–3–3–1 distribution. He can therefore play ♣K and confidently finesse against East.

DISTRIBUTION
1 The way in which the 13 cards of a suit are dispersed amongst the four hands.
2 The way in which the four suits are arranged within one hand. For example: 5–4–3–1 'distribution.' This is also called the hand's 'pattern' or 'shape'.

DISTRIBUTIONAL POINT COUNT
Points based on distribution which can be added to the High Card Points value of a hand in order to improve the estimation of its playing strength. A number of methods are in use, some based on shortages, others on length. For example:
1 The Goren Count (or 3–2–1 count) adds three points for a void, two for a singleton and one for a doubleton.
2 The Karpin Count adds points not for shortages, but for extra length in the bid suit, one extra point for each card over four in the longest suit; so a five-card suit gains one point, a six-card suit gains two extra points, etc. The Karpin count is used by opener in evaluating his hand. In responding, with primary

trump support, the 5–3–1 count is more accurate while the
3–2–1 count is used with only secondary support.
While the shortage and length points' methods produce similar
results, both may be improved somewhat with the following
additions:
   With a singleton King, Queen or Jack, deduct one point.
   With five trumps in the responding hand, add one point.

DISTRIBUTIONAL VALUE
A holding of worth, due to shortage or length in suits. See
DISTRIBUTIONAL POINT COUNT

DIXON CONVENTION
First recognized defence to the Multi, based on the principle that a
double of 2◇ shows a fairly balanced hand of about 13–16 points,
immediate overcalls of 2♡ and 2♠ show the equivalent of a take
out double of the other major and other bids are natural. See
DEFENCE TO MULTI, MULTICOLOURED TWO DIAMOND
OPENER

DOPE/ROPE
Conventions used after intervention following a Blackwood 4NT,
allowing responder to show an even number of Aces or an odd
number of Aces. After an intervening bid, **D**ouble shows an **O**dd
number of Aces, **P**ass an **E**ven number. After an intervening
double, **R**edouble shows an **O**dd number of Aces and **P**ass an
Even number.

DOPI/ROPI
Conventions used after intervention following a Blackwood 4NT.
Following an intervening bid, **D**ouble shows zero (**O**) Aces, **P**ass
one (**I**) and other responses on a step principle, the first step (e.g.
5♡ after a 5◇ overcall) showing two Aces etc. After an intervening
double, **R**edouble shows zero (**O**) Aces, **P**ass one (**I**) Ace etc. See
PODI, PORI

DOUBLE
A call that increases the value of tricks bid and made, the penalty

for undertricks, the bonuses for overtricks, and will lead to an additional bonus of 50 points if the doubled contract is successful. The call is used conventionally for several purposes. See COMPETITIVE, CO-OPERATIVE, DOUBLE OF THREE NO TRUMP BIDS, LIGHTNER, NEGATIVE, PENALTY, RESPONSIVE, TAKE OUT, UNPENALTY

DOUBLE DUMMY
A play in a particular situation which could not possibly be bettered even if declarer could see all four hands. To examine a hand double dummy is to look at all four hands simultaneously. A double dummy problem is one in which all four hands are displayed.

DOUBLE FINESSE
A finesse against two outstanding honours. For example:

```
            A Q 10
          ┌───────┐
          │   N   │
    K J 8 │ W   E │ 9 7 6 2
          │   S   │
          └───────┘
             5 4 3
```

South must first finesse the 10, and then the Queen to take all three tricks.

DOUBLE JUMP OVERCALL
An overcall skipping two levels of bidding (e.g. 1♡–3♠).

DOUBLE JUMP RAISE
A raise missing out two levels of bidding. It is usually pre-emptive in nature, e.g. 1♡–4♡.

DOUBLE NEGATIVE
In the sequence 2♣–NB–2◊–NB–2♡/2♠–NB–2NT, most partnerships agree that the 2NT bid is a second negative, showing a very poor hand.

DOUBLE OF THREE NO TRUMP BIDS

When the opponents bid to 3NT, a double by the defender who will not be on lead is usually played as lead directing asking for a particular lead, often dummy's first bid suit. If both defenders have bid a different suit, the double asks partner to lead his own suit rather than that of the doubler. If no suit has been bid, a double shows a long solid suit and asks partner to lead his shortest suit.

DOUBLE RAISE

A raise of opener's suit by two levels (e.g. 1♠–NB–3♠). In Acol this is a limit raise usually showing 4-card support and 10–12 points. See INVERTED MINOR SUIT RAISES

DOUBLE SQUEEZE

See SQUEEZE

DOUBLED INTO GAME

A player is said to have been doubled into game if an opponent has doubled his contract and the score for the tricks made, if the contract is successful, will exceed 100 while this score would have been less than 100 had the contract not been doubled. For example, to double a contract of 2♠ would be to double into game but to double a contract of 2◇ would not.

DOUBLER

The person who doubles.

DOUBLETON

A holding of only two cards in a suit.

DOWN

Failing to make the contracted number of tricks.

DRAWING TRUMPS

The act of playing successive rounds of trumps in order to remove the opponents' trumps.

DRIVE OUT

To force out an opponent's high card by leading a sufficiently high card in the same suit and continuing the suit until the outstanding high card is played.

DROP
To play a high card and cause an opponent to play another missing high card, as in the expression: 'to drop the singleton King offside.'

DRURY CONVENTION
A conventional 2♣ response to a third- or fourth-hand opening asking if the opener has a sound or sub-minimum opener.

DUCK
To decline to take a trick that could have been won.

DUKE OF CUMBERLAND'S HAND
Dealt to the son of George IV at whist. Clubs were trumps and the Duke held:

   ♠ A K Q
   ♡ A K Q J
   ◇ A K
   ♣ K J 9 7

His opponents bet that he would not make a single trick in his hand. According to the story, he accepted the bet and lost all thirteen tricks. The complete deal was:

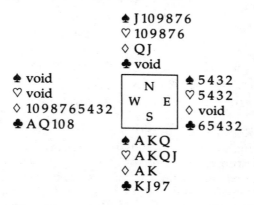

        ♠ J 10 9 8 7 6
        ♡ 10 9 8 7 6
        ◇ Q J
        ♣ void

♠ void   ♠ 5 4 3 2
♡ void   N   ♡ 5 4 3 2
◇ 10 9 8 7 6 5 4 3 2 W E ◇ void
♣ A Q 10 8   S   ♣ 6 5 4 3 2

        ♠ A K Q
        ♡ A K Q J
        ◇ A K
        ♣ K J 9 7

Following whist principles of the time, the Duke led the ♣7 of. The lead was won with the ♣8, and after two diamond ruffs and two further club leads through the Duke, the last trump was drawn and the seven remaining diamonds cashed.

DUMB BIDDER

Device to permit silent bidding. It is a board placed in the centre of the table, subdivided into labelled regions, 1♣, 1◊, 1♡, 1♠, 1NT, 2♣ etc. (up to 7NT), **DBL**, **RDBL**, **ALERT**, **STOP** and **NO BID**. A player makes his call by touching the appropriate region of the board with a pen or pencil, or moving a small counter placed on the dumb bidder.

DUMMY

1 The partner of the declarer.
2 The hand of the partner of the declarer.

DUMMY REVERSAL

A method of play by which the hand with longer trumps (declarer) is used to ruff losers in dummy. Dummy's trumps are then used to draw the remaining trumps. Here is an example:

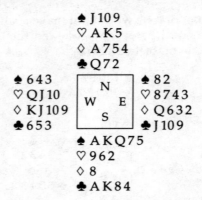

South is in a contract of 7♠, but has only eleven top tricks. Declarer can get home however, when the black suits break evenly, by means of a dummy reversal. If dummy's three losing diamonds are ruffed with declarer's top trumps, South ends up with three trump tricks, four club tricks, three tricks from the red suit winners and three tricks by trumping diamonds in hand.

DUPLICATE BRIDGE

A form of bridge in which each board is played several times by different players. The luck of the deal is thus eliminated since players' scores are compared with the other results on each board. The first application of the duplicate principle was in Duplicate Whist by John T. Mitchell, inventor of the first pairs movement. Duplicate Auction Bridge was first played in 1914 under the auspices of the American Whist League.

DUPLICATION OF DISTRIBUTION

A duplication of distribution is said to occur when both players have exactly the same length in each suit. It is also called 'Mirror distribution'.

DUPLICATION OF VALUES

A duplication of values is said to occur when both players have a strong holding in a particular suit with the result that, whilst the combined honour point strength is high, the trick-taking potential is limited.

♠ A Q 4	♠ K J 3
♡ K Q 6	♡ A J 7
◇ 7 6 4 2	◇ K J 8 3
♣ K J 4	♣ 7 3 2

Whilst East–West hold a combined 28 high-card points, they can only take six certain tricks.

—E—

EAST

One of the positions at the bridge table.

EBU

See ENGLISH BRIDGE UNION

ECHO
The play by a defender of an unnecessarily high card on the first round of a suit followed by a lower card on the second round is occasionally called an 'echo'. It is more commonly known as a 'peter' or 'high-low' and is used as a signal to partner that he likes the suit, or that he has an even number of cards in it. See REVERSE PETER, SMITH PETER

ELIMINATION
The process of removing neutral cards from defenders' hands in order that they have no safe exit when they are thrown in (given the lead).

EN PASSANT
See COUP EN PASSANT

ENCOURAGING
A term applied to a bid or a card which urges partner to bid on or to continue leading a suit.

ENDPLAY
A term used when an opponent is given the lead at a vital stage of the play and, with his subsequent lead, is forced to concede a trick or tricks and is therefore 'endplayed'. The vital point is more likely to occur in the end stage of the play. For example:

```
                ♡ 9
                ◇ A 6 5
          ┌───────────┐
    ♡ Q   │     N     │   ♡ 8
    ◇ QJ9 │  W     E  │   ◇ 8 3 2
          │     S     │
          └───────────┘
                ♡ 7
                ◇ K 10 4
```

South, on play in No Trumps, needs three of the last four tricks. If he leads a diamond, West is certain to win two tricks. Instead, he uses an 'endplay' by putting West on lead with ♡Q. West is now 'endplayed' and is forced to lead diamonds, conceding all three tricks.

ENGLISH BRIDGE UNION
Regulatory body for Duplicate Bridge in England.

ENTRY
A card that can be used to enter a particular hand.

ENTRY KILLING PLAY
A defensive manoeuvre designed to destroy entries either in declarer's hand, or in dummy. See MERRIMAC COUP, SCISSORS COUP

EQUALS
A holding of cards in sequence at the start of play, or of the same value as the play progresses, is said to be a holding of 'equals'.

ESCAPE MECHANISM
A bidding device used to locate the safest fit after the opponents have doubled for penalties. Often applied after the double of a weak or mini No Trump opening. See WRIGGLE

ESCAPE SUIT
A suit held in reserve by a player making a psychic bid. For a regular systemic bid with an escape suit, see GAMBLING 3NT

ESTABLISHED CARD
A card that has been established as a winner.

ESTABLISHED ENTRY
An entry which has been established.

ESTABLISHED REVOKE
A revoke becomes established (i.e. it cannot be corrected) when one of the offending side leads or plays to the next trick. A revoke on the twelfth trick cannot be established.

ESTABLISHED SUIT
A suit where a partnership holds all the remaining high cards.

ETHICS
The Proprieties of the game as distinct from the actual Laws. See
LAWS AND ETHICS COMMITTEE

ETIQUETTE
In general, good manners at the bridge table. (For example,
declarer thanking partner when dummy is faced).

EVEN
1 Term applied to an even division of the outstanding cards (3–3
   is the even break with six cards outstanding; 4–3 an even
   distribution of seven).
2 An even card is one with an even number of pips (2, 4, 6 etc.).

EXHAUST
To draw all the outstanding cards in a suit from a particular hand.

EXIT
To surrender the lead.

EXIT CARD
A card used to exit in the hope of a favourable return or a safe card
with which to exit. See THROW IN

EXPLANATION OF BID
If a player is asked to explain his partner's bid, he should fully
explain the partnership agreement according to the system being
played. It is wrong to offer an explanation of what the bid ought to
mean, or to say how one proposes to interpret it. If the partnership
has no agreement (explicit or implicit) then the player should say
so. An explanation must not be offered unless opponents ask.

EXPOSED CARD
A card wrongly or inadvertently exposed during the auction or
play.

EXPOSED HAND
1 The dummy.

2 Declarer or a defender may expose their hand when making a
   claim.

EXTENDED STAYMAN
After a 2◊ response to the 2♣ enquiry, a further enquiry bid of 3◊
asks about three-card major suits. In reply:

   3♡   Shows three hearts and two spades.
   3♠   Shows three spades and two hearts.
   3NT Shows two spades and two hearts.
   4♣   Shows three cards in both majors.

See STAYMAN CONVENTION

FACE
To turn a card so that its front is visible to the other players. See
FACED LEAD

FACED LEAD
In duplicate bridge, the opening lead must be made face down.
This is to allow partner to ask questions regarding the auction
without influencing the choice of lead. When these questions are
completed the card is turned over or 'faced'.

FACTORING
The process of adjusting a matchpoint score. If, for example, some
pairs have played fewer boards than the rest of the field then their
scores must be factored up by the appropriate fraction.
Alternatively the scores of the pairs playing more boards may be
factored down. See MATCHPOINT(S)

FALL OF THE CARDS
The disposition of the cards as ordained by fate.

FALSE CARDING
Deceptive play of a card in the hope that the opposition will
misread the holding in the suit.

FALSE PREFERENCE
After partner has bid two suits responder may choose to play in the first suit bid despite the fact that he is longer in the second. See PREFERENCE

FARRINGTON, FRANK
Author of the first book of Duplicate Bridge Movements, considered the definitive work on the subject.

FEATURE
A holding in a suit, such as the Ace, King, or sometimes the Queen, which is likely to be important on the given hand.

FIELDING A PSYCHE
If a player makes a psychic bid and his partner takes a subsequent action based on the fact that the first player has psyched, then he is said to have 'fielded' the psyche. To 'field' a psyche is not in itself illegal if, either the subsequent auction has clearly exposed partner's psyche, or if the call which 'fields' the psyche is clearly the normal action anyway. To 'field' a psyche before it has clearly been exposed by taking an abnormal action is illegal. See PSYCHIC BID

FIFTH ACE
As the trump King is often as important as an Ace, some conventions treat the King of trumps as the 'fifth' Ace. See FIVE ACE BLACKWOOD

FILM
A conventional defence to an opening pre-emptive three level bid. The acronym stands for **FI**shbein and **L**ower **M**inor. Over an opening 3◊ or 3♡ bid, Fishbein (the next suit up) is a take-out request guaranteeing at least four cards in the bid major, and 4♣ is for take out denying four cards in the bid major. Over an opening 3♣ or 3♠ bid, the lower minor is a take out request. See DEFENCE TO OPENING THREE BID, FISHBEIN, LOWER MINOR

FINAL BID
The last bid before three consecutive passes end the auction.

FINESSE
An attempt to win a trick with the lower ranking card when leading towards a tenace. For example:

A Q

3 2

If West has the King, this suit will yield two tricks if South leads towards the tenace, playing the Queen unless the King appears. A finesse position arises in a number of different forms but all of them depend on the assumption that a particular card or cards may be held in a certain hand. See CHINESE FINESSE, DEEP FINESSE, DOUBLE FINESSE, FREE FINESSE, REPEATED FINESSE, RUFFING FINESSE

FIRST IN HAND
The dealer, the first player to have the opportunity to open the bidding.

FISHBEIN CONVENTION
The use of a bid of the next higher-ranking suit (e.g. 3♡–3♠) after a three-level pre-emptive opening bid as a take-out request. Sometimes called 'Herbert'. It will normally provide at least four cards in the suit bid.

FISHBOWL
Method of allowing tournament bridge to be viewed by an audience. The players sit inside a large glass surround, enabling the spectators to watch without disturbing the players.

FISHING CLUB
See PHONEY CLUB

FIT

1 The combined holding in a suit.
2 The two hands of a partnership are said to fit well if, for instance, one player has only small cards (hence no wasted values) in a side suit in which his partner is void.

FIVE ACE BLACKWOOD

A version of Blackwood in which the King of the agreed trump suit is treated as a fifth Ace. In response to 4NT:

5♣ Shows zero or three Aces
5♦ Shows one or four Aces
5♥ Shows two Aces
5♠ Shows five Aces

FIVE-CARD MAJORS

Some systems require that an opening bid of 1♥ or 1♠ guarantees at least a five-card suit.

FIVE-CARD SPADES

Some systems require that an opening of 1♠ guarantees five cards, but 1♥ does not.

FIVE-CARD STAYMAN

After a 1NT or 2NT opening bid, 2♣ or 3♣ asks partner to bid a five-card major. The diamond response denies the holding. If responder has a four-card major he now bids it and opener will confirm a 4–4 major suit fit if one exists.

FIVE OF A MAJOR OPENING

This conventional opening shows an eleven playing-trick hand missing both top trump honours. Responder passes with neither top honour, raises to six with one of the two top honours, and to seven with both top honours.

FIVE SUIT BRIDGE

A game devised in 1937 by Dr Marculis of Vienna, using a 65-card deck containing 5 suits of 13 cards each. It did not achieve lasting popularity.

FIXED
A colloquialism meaning that a pair has received a bad score through no fault of its own.

FLAT BOARD
In duplicate pairs, a hand on which the same result was scored by all the contestants. In teams, a hand on which both sides recorded the same score.

FLAT HAND
A balanced hand, particularly the 4–3–3–3 pattern.

FLINT CONVENTION
A convention invented by the English player, Jeremy Flint, designed to allow the partnership to play in three of a major after an opening bid of 2NT. Immediate responses of 3♡ and 3♠ remain natural and forcing, promising at least five cards but 3◊ is used artificially to ask opener to bid 3♡. With long hearts and a weak hand responder now passes; with long spades he converts to 3♠. Nowadays Flint has been superseded by Transfer Bids.

FLITCH
Competition for married couples.

FLOGGER
Sheet recording the results of previous rubbers.

FORCE
1 To make a forcing bid.
2 To make an opponent ruff in order to shorten trumps in one of the hands. It is often used as a defensive manoeuvre.

FORCED BID
A bid that a player is forced to make, usually because the system that is being played so requires.

FORCING DEFENCE
Strategy whereby the defenders keep playing cards which

declarer must ruff until declarer runs out of trumps and the defenders gain control.

FORCING 1NT
A convention whereby a response of 1NT to an opening of one of a major is forcing for one round. It is usually used in conjunction with strong two-over-one responses (10/11+ points).

FORCING BID
A bid which requires partner to make at least one further bid.

FORCING PASS
1 A pass which forces partner to bid or to double. Often when a player has to make the decision between doubling a sacrifice bid made by an opponent or bidding on himself, he may pass and let his partner make the final decision.
2 Systems utilizing the opening call of 'No bid' as a positive bid.

FORCING SEQUENCE
A bidding sequence, which by partnership agreement, is forcing.

FORCING TO GAME
See GAME FORCING BID

FORCING TWO BID
The use of an opening two-level bid as an unconditional, natural game force. See ACOL TWO BID, STRONG TWO BID

FORFEIT
Cancellation of rights, as appropriate under the Laws, after a misdemeanour.

FORWARD GOING
A description of an encouraging bid.

FOULED BOARD
A board in which the hands have been misplaced, and which cannot be played at the next table.

FOUR-CARD MAJORS
Systems which do not guarantee more than four cards in the suit when a major suit is opened.

FOUR CLUB BLACKWOOD
See GERBER

FOUR DEAL BRIDGE
See CHICAGO

FOUR NO TRUMP CONVENTION
A bid with various artificial meanings.
See ACOL, BLACKWOOD, BYZANTINE BLACKWOOD, CULBERTSON 4–5 NT, FIVE ACE BLACKWOOD, GENERAL PURPOSE CUE BID, NORMAN, ROMAN BLACKWOOD, ROMAN KEY-CARD BLACKWOOD

FOURTH-HIGHEST LEAD
The lead of the fourth highest card in a suit. This is the standard lead unless the suit contains no honour or contains an honour sequence. See RULE OF ELEVEN

FOURTH IN HAND
The player who is fourth to call, i.e. the player to the dealer's right.

FOURTH-SUIT FORCING
After a partnership has bid three suits, it is unlikely that the fourth suit is the best fit. Therefore a bid of the fourth suit can usefully be played as an artificial one round force asking partner to describe his hand further. The bid does not promise any particular holding in the bid suit.

FOXU
A conventional defence to an opening three level pre-emptive bid. FISHBEIN is employed sitting Over the bidder and double (X) sitting Under, as take out requests. See DEFENCE TO OPENING THREE BID

FRAGMENT BID

An unusual jump or double jump bid showing a fit for partner's suit and a shortage in the fourth suit. See SPLINTER BID

FREAK

A hand or complete deal with an extremely abnormal distribution.

FREE BID

A 'free bid' is one which is made by a player after his right hand opponent has overcalled his partner's bid. The overcall ensures that his partner will have another chance to bid and therefore the player has the option of passing. A 'free bid' in a new suit will normally show better than minimum values.

FREE DOUBLE

At rubber bridge it refers to the double of a game bid (or a partscore contract which, if successful would make game whether doubled, undoubled or redoubled). It is not of course 'free' but is likely to be less costly than doubling the opposition into game.

FREE FINESSE

Term used to describe a finesse declarer can take without being disadvantaged should it fail. For example:

♡ K J 2

♡ A 3

West leads a heart and South finesses the ♡J.

FRIGID

Slang term for a contract which is certain to make. 'Cold' and 'Icy' are similar terms.

FRUIT MACHINE SWISS
See SWISS CONVENTION

GADGET
A convention or part of a convention.

GAMBIT
The deliberate sacrifice of a trick in order to gain two or more tricks as a result.

GAMBLING 3NT
An opening bid of 3NT to show a long and solid minor, at least A K Q x x x x, with no more than an outside Queen.

GAME
The 100 points scored below the line in rubber bridge. 100 or more trick points scored on one deal in duplicate bridge.

GAME ALL
In rubber bridge when both sides have previously won a game and are thus both vulnerable. In duplicate or Chicago when the pre-determined vulnerability so indicates.

GAME BID
A bid of just enough tricks to make game: 3NT, four of a major or five of a minor. In rubber bridge, if the partnership already has points towards game, the bid may be at a level sufficient to convert that partscore into game.

GAME CONTRACT
Any contract which if successful will yield enough tricks to make game.

GAME DEMAND BID
See GAME FORCING BID

GAME FORCING BID
A bid which demands that the partnership does not stop short of the game.

GAME FORCING SITUATION
A sequence of bidding which has committed both members of a partnership to reach a game contract.

GAME HOG
A player who habitually distorts his own bidding for the purpose of being declarer in game contracts.

GAME IN
Another expression for 'Vulnerable'.

GAME INVITATION
A bid which does not force the partnership to game but invites partner to bid it with extra values, in the context of his previous bidding.

GAME TRY DOUBLE
A double made in competitive auction, when both sides have bid and supported a suit as a means of distinguishing between a competitive raise of partner's suit and a game invitation. The double is the game invitation, and the immediate raise is thus purely competitive.

GARBAGE
Slang term for a poor hand.

GARDENER 1NT OVERCALL
An overcall of 1NT to show either a stron no trump (15–17 or 16–18 points) or a weak hand with a long suit.

GENERAL LICENCE
Licensing a category of the EBU laws and Ethics Committee relating to treatments and conventions that are approved for most competitions. See RESTRICTED LICENCE

GENERAL PURPOSE CUE BID
A bid of 4NT used as a general slam try when a cue bid is not available or convenient.

GERBER

A convention whereby a bid of 4♣ asks about the nuber of Aces held by partner. In reponse:

4◇	Shows zero or four Aces
4♡	Shows one Ace
4♠	Shows two Aces
4NT	Shows three Aces

Subsequently 5♣ enquires about Kings with corresponding responses.

GESTURE

A remark or mannerism that suggests a call, lead, or play.

GET A COUNT OF THE HAND

To discover the distribution of the unseen hands either as declarer or defender.

GHESTEM

A system of strong two-suited overcalls devised by Pierre Ghestem of France:

Over 1◇/1♡/1♠:	2NT	Shows the lowest two unbid suits
	3♣	Shows the highest two unbid suits
	Cue bid	Shows the other two suits
Over 1♣:	2NT	Shows the red suits
	2◇	Shows the majors
	3♣	Shows the other suits (diamonds and spades)

The modification after an opening 1♣ bid was introduced to allow an overcall of 2♣ to be natural because, in France, a 1♣ opening is frequently made on a three-card suit. Another modification of the Ghestem convetion uses the cue bid after a minor suit opening to show the extreme suits (spades and the other minor) and the jump cue bid (e.g. 1♣–3♣) to show the majors.

GIN

Slang term meaning that a contract is certain to succeed.

GIVE COUNT

To make a distributional signal.

GLADIATOR

A system of esponses to a 1NT opener: 2♣ demands 2◇ which reponder can pass or convert to 2♡ or 2♠. 2◇ is now the Stayman enquiry (2NT denying a four-card major), 2♡ and 2♠ now game forcing with a five-card suit. A jump to three of a major is now a slam invitation.

GO DOWN

To make fewer tricks than contracted for.

GO IN

A defender in second position who plays the Ace when declarer leads low towards dummy is said to 'go in' or 'go up' with the Ace.

GO OFF

To make fewer tricks than contracted for.

GO TO GAME

To bid a game.

GO UP

See GO IN

GOLD CUP

The premier Knock-Out Team Championship of Great Britain, contested under the auspices of the British Bridge League.

GOOD

Adjective used to describe a hand in which every card is a winner, e.g. 'Dummy is good'. 'High' is used in the same sense.

GOREN, Charles H

American bridge player, successful in converting the bridge playing world from honour tricks to point valuation and founder of much modern American bidding theory. See STANDARD AMERICAN

GOREN SYSTEM

See STANDARD AMERICAN

GOULASH

A method of dealing when the cards are not shuffled after the initial deal and play. Five cards are dealt at once in turn to each player. This is repeated for a second round, before a further three cards are dealt at once to each player. As one might expect, hands dealt this way are often wildly distributional.

GRAND COUP

A trump coup in which winners must be ruffed to shorten declarer's trumps. The name comes from the early days of whist when it was then thought that such a play deserved a high-sounding title.

GRAND MASTER

The highest Master Point rank of a National Bridge Union.

GRAND SLAM

To bid a Grand Slam is to contract to make all thirteen tricks. See BONUS

GRAND SLAM FORCE

A convention invented by Ely and Josephine Culbertson but first published by Josephine in the Bridge World and hence often referred to as 'Josephine', whereby a direct bid of 5NT (not preceded by 4NT) after a trump suit has been agreed asks partner how many of the three top trumps honours (Ace, King and Queen) he holds. Originally responder bid seven of the trump suit with two or three top honours and six of the trump suit with none or one. More sophisticated methods have since been devised to give better definition. For example:

    6♣ No top honour
    6◇ One top honour
    6♡ Two top honours
    6♠ Three top honours
See MODIFIED GRAND SLAM FORCE

GREEK GIFT

A trick offered to the opposition which, if accepted, leads to disaster.

GREEN

1 One of the traffic-light terms used by the Laws and Ethics Committee of the English Bridge Union to categorize psychic bids. A 'green' psyche is one where the partnership's subsequent actions provide no evidence of an unauthorized partnership understanding. See AMBER, PSYCHIC BID, RED
2 Shorthand for describing the vulnerability of both partnerships on a board and meaning that the 'green' partnership is not vulnerable but their opponents are vulnerable. See AMBER, RED, WHITE

GREEN POINTS

National Master Points issued by the English Bridge Union (for success in certain larger tournaments. Their accumulation is necessary to attain the higher grades in its ranking system. See LOCAL POINTS, MASTER POINTS, RANK, RANKING SYSTEMS, RED POINTS

GROSVENOR COUP

An intentional misplay which would allow an opponent to gain an extra trick but which is so 'stupid' that the opponent will never believe the misplay has occurred. For example:

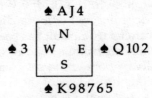

♠ A J 4

	N	
♠ 3	W E	♠ Q 10 2
	S	

♠ K 9 8 7 6 5

North cashes the ♠A and then leads the ♠J. East plays a 'Grosvenor Coup' by following with the two then ten. South will never believe that East has failed to play the Queen on the Jack and so will play his king hoping for a 2–2 break.

GUARD

A card combination which prevents the opposition from immediately running tricks in a suit.

GUARD SQUEEZE

A triple squeeze in which one opponent holds stoppers in two suits with a guard to a finesse against his partner in a third suit, for example:

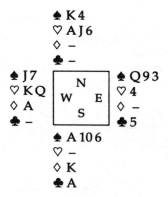

When South leads ♣A, West is squeezed in three suits. He has stoppers in hearts and diamonds and a guard in spades. He is forced to discard a spade, thus enabling South to play spades and take the finesse against East. See SQUEEZE

GUIDE CARD

A card used to instruct contestants to which table they should move after the end of each round, either given to each contestant, or placed on each table.

—H—

HACKETT

A defence to weak two openings whereby 3♣ is a take-out request showing less than 16 points, 3◊ is a take-out request showing 16+ points.

HALF TABLE

A table at which only one pair is sitting.

HALF TRICK
An honour holding which can be expected to win a trick half the time such as K x, or the Queen is a holding of A Q (one and a half tricks).

HAND
1. The thirteen cards held by a player
2. The set of four hands
3. The position at the table, as in 'First in hand' (the dealer).

HAND PATTERN
The way in which the four suits are arranged within one hand. For example: 5–4–3–1 'pattern'. This is also called the hand's 'distribution' or 'shape'.

HANDICAPPING
To impose a penalty on the stronger members of the field so as to allow the weaker players a chance of victory.

HARD VALUES
Aces and Kings. By comparison Queens and Jacks are called 'soft values'.

HERBERT DEFENCE TO WEAK THREES
See FISHBEIN

HERBERT NEGATIVE
A bid of the next step up (e.g. 2♡–NB–2♠) as a negative response to strong two opening bid. Over 2♠ some players use 2NT as the negative response, others 3♣.

HESITATION
The proprieties of bridge dictate that bidding and play should be made in even tempo and rhythm. An unusually long pause by a player before bidding or playing to a trick would be undue hesitation. The player's partner then has an obligation under the Laws to ignore any unauthorized information gained from such hesitation.

HEXAGON SQUEEZE

Otherwise known as a Double Guard Squeeze, in which each of the three menaces is protected by both opponents.

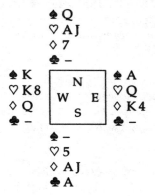

In this example, when South leads ♣A, West must discard ♠K and dummy discards a diamond. East is now squeezed in three suits. See SQUEEZE

HIDDEN ENTRY

A low card, usually in the dummy, by which an entry can be made. It is established by declarer playing his high cards of a suit under the high cards in dummy.

HIGH

See GOOD

HIGH CARD

1 An Ace, King, Queen or Jack.
2 A card that has become established.

HIGH CARD POINTS (HCPs)

Numerical measure of hand's playing and defensive strength counting an Ace as four points, a King as three, a Queen as two and a Jack as one and discounting distributional points.

HIGH-LOW SIGNAL
The play by a defender of an unnecessarily high card on the first round of a suit followed by a lower card on the second round to signal to partner. Usually the peter is used to show that the signaller likes the suit or that he has an even number of cards in the suit. The signal is also known as an 'echo' or 'peter'. See REVERSE PETER, SMITH PETER

HIGH REVERSE
A rebid by opener in a lower ranking new suit at the three level after a two over one response, e.g. 1♠–NB–2♣–NB–3♣. It is a bid which is normally played as forcing to game.

HINDSIGHT
Frequently expressed by players in their post mortem of hands which they might have bid or played better. See RESULTS MERCHANT

HIT
Colloquialism for double.

HOBSON'S COUP
See MERRIMAC COUP

HOG
A person who attempts to become the declarer as often as possible. Thus the phrase 'to hog the bidding'.

HOLD UP
Decline to win a trick, often with the intention of disrupting opponents' communications.

HOLDING
Particular cards in a player's hand, as in 'A good club holding'.

HONEYMOON BRIDGE
A somewhat unlikely term to describe various forms of two-handed bridge.

HONOUR
One of the five highest cards in a suit, i.e. the Ace, King, Queen, Jack or 10.

HONOUR LEAD
The lead of an honour card.

HONOUR STRENGTH
The value of a hand in terms of honour cards.

HONOUR TRICKS
As defined by Culbertson, an honour trick was the basic unit of defensive value. The overall value of a hand was calculated by totalling the number of honour tricks in each suit:

A K	Two honour tricks
A Q	One and a half honour tricks
A K Q, K J 10	One honour trick
K x, Q J x	Half an honour trick

In addition 'plus values' were deemed to be worth approximately one quarter of an honour trick. Plus values were: Any Queen which was not a singleton, any Jack supported by another honour (but not a doubleton combination nor in a suit holding of A K Q J), any singleton or void (but not more than one).

HONOURS
In rubber bridge or Chicago any player holding four or five honour cards in the trump suit or holding all four Aces in a no trump contract may claim for 'Honours' and score a bonus. See BONUS

HOOK
To finesse.

HOUSE PLAYER
A player at a rubber bridge club 'employed' by the management to make up tables.

HOUSE RULES
Additions or amendments to the Laws as required to meet the conditions of play in a club or group. Such rules would apply mainly to matters of dress, periods of play, stake limits etc.

HOWELL
Cyclic pairs movement, usually dictated by movement cards, allowing competitive play with as few as three tables. Unlike Mitchell movements pairs change directions at some tables. In a full Howell movement all the pairs will play all the other pairs. See MITCHELL, THREE QUARTER MOVEMENT

HOYLE, Edmond
First codifier of the rules of Whist. His famous work of 1742, briefly entitled *A Short Treatise on the Game of Whist Containing the Laws of the Game and also Some Rules Whereby a Beginner May, with Due Attention to them, Attain to the Playing It Well*, became a bestseller.

HUDDLE
A prolonged hesitation.

HUM
With the advent of many weird and wonderful systems and conventions, the Laws have deemed some as: 'Highly Unusual Methods' or HUMs.

HYBRID SCORING
A form of scoring which combines the best features of IMP scoring and point-a-board scoring. Used in top-level contests, where two teams play only short matches.

ICY
Slang term for a contract which is certain to make. 'Cold' and 'Frigid' are similar terms.

IDLE CARD
A card not required for a specific purpose as distinct from a busy card. The term usually applies to unimportant cards in squeeze positions.

ILLEGAL CALL
A call in the course of the bidding auction which is insufficient, out of rotation, or otherwise improper.

IMP
See INTERNATIONAL MATCH POINTS (IMPs)

IMPOSSIBLE NEGATIVE
In response to a Precision one-club opening, 4–4–4–1 hands with positive values are shown by initially giving the systemic negative response of 1◊ and subsequently making a bid inconsistent with the holding of negative values, thus indicating an 'impossible negative'.

IMPROPRIETY
A breach of ethical conduct.

IN FRONT OF
Term describing the position of a player with respect to his left-hand opponent and therefore having to play before him.

INCOMPLETE RUBBER
If a game of bridge has to be terminated before the end of a rubber, bonuses are awarded depending on the state of the rubber. For scoring, see BONUS

INCOMPLETE TABLE
A table at which fewer than the necessary four players are sitting, and especially a half table at duplicate.

INDIVIDUAL MOVEMENT
A movement used in an event where individual players score separately, competing with different partners against one another.

INFERENCE
A conclusion drawn about the likely lie of the cards from the previous play and bidding.

INFORMATORY DOUBLE
Old term for take out double. See TAKE OUT DOUBLE

INHIBITORY DOUBLE
A psychic manoeuvre which is generally considered to be unethical because nowadays it succeeds only against inexperienced players.

INSPECTION OF TRICKS
In rubber bridge any player may inspect the previous trick until his side has played to the next trick. In duplicate he may not do so after he has turned his own card over. He may however inspect, but not expose, his own card until a card has been led to the next trick.

INSTANT MATCHPOINTING
A method of scoring hands as if they had been played in a duplicate event by comparing the score obtained with a pre-determined chart.

INSUFFICIENT BID
A bid not legally sufficient, i.e. below the level of the minimum allowable bid. The Laws apply.

INSULT
The bonus of 50 (100) points awarded for bidding and making a doubled (redoubled) contract is commonly referred to as '50 (100) for the insult'. See BONUS

INSURANCE BID
Sacrifice bid against a high level contract by the opposition despite some expectation of defeating that contract.

INTERFERENCE BID
Any defensive overcall made to obstruct the opponents' bidding. It is not strength-showing or attacking. Jump bids are often used effectively for pre-emptive interference.

INTERIOR SEQUENCE
A sequence of honour cards (but including the 9) comprising two or more touching cards with one higher non-touching honour. For example, A J 10 9, K J 10, Q 10 9.

INTERMEDIATE CARDS
Tens, nines and eights.

INTERMEDIATE JUMP OVERCALLS
A jump overcall based on a good opening hand with a six card-suit.

INTERNATIONAL BRIDGE PRESS ASSOCIATION (IBPA)
A worldwide organization whose members are either bridge authors or newspaper columnists.

INTERNATIONAL MATCH POINTS (IMPs)
A method of scoring used in teams matches whereby the aggregate difference between the scores of opposing teams on each board is converted to International Match Points on a defined sliding scale. The purpose is to allow large swings to be rewarded more generously than small ones but to limit the extent of very large swings to prevent the result on one board effectively determining the outcome of an entire match. In certain events a further conversion is made to Victory Points. See VICTORY POINTS, MATCHPOINTS

Aggregate Difference	IMP Difference	Aggregate Difference	IMP Difference
0–10	0	130–160	4
20–40	1	170–210	5
50–80	2	220–260	6
90–120	3	270–310	7

Aggregate Difference	IMP Difference	Aggregate Difference	IMP Difference
320–360	8	1500–1740	17
370–420	9	1750–1990	18
430–490	10	2000–2240	19
500–590	11	2250–2490	20
600–740	12	2500–2990	21
750–890	13	3000–3490	22
900–1090	14	3500–3990	23
1100–1290	15	4000+	24
1300–1490	16		

INTERVENING BID
An overcall.

INVERTED MINOR SUIT RAISES
This convention 'inverts' the normal meanings of the single and double raises of a minor suit. Thus 1◊–NB–2◊ is stronger than 1◊–NB–3◊.

INVITATIONAL BID
A bid that encourages partner to bid on, holding any extra values in the context of his previous bidding.

ISOLATING THE MENACE
A method of leaving only one player in the position of guarding a particular suit, thus increasing the chance of executing a successful squeeze. See SQUEEZE, THREAT CARD (MENACE)

—J—

JACOBY TRANSFER BIDS
Invented by Oswald Jacoby, a response of 2◊ (2♡) over an opening 1NT shows at least five cards in hearts (spades). See TRANSFER BIDS

JETTISON
To discard a high honour (usually Ace or King), often to create an entry for partner or to unblock a suit.

JOSEPHINE
See GRAND SLAM FORCE

JOURNALIST LEADS
A complete system of opening leads as follows:
Against no trumps:
Ace from a strong holding (e.g. A K J x or A K 10 x).
King from a weaker holding.
Queen from Q J x or a weak K Q x holding.
Jack from J 10, but no higher honour.
10 from an interior sequence (e.g. A J 10 x or K 10 9 x).
9 from 10 9 x.
Lowest from a suit headed by an honour (but not one of the above honour combinations).
Second highest from suits without an honour.
Against a suit contract:
Lower of two touching honours.
Third and fifth from an honour or non-touching honours.
Top of nothing.

JUMP BID
Any bid at a level higher than necessary to show the denomination. See STOP

JUMP OVERCALL
A single jump bid made as an overcall.

JUMP PREFERENCE
To return partner to his original suit at the same time making a jump bid.

JUMP SHIFT
A single jump in a new suit by responder. The bid is normally forcing to at least game unless made by a passed hand. In the latter

case it promises near opening values, a fair suit and primary support for opener.

JUNIOR
In international competition, a player under the age of 25.

JUNK
A worthless hand or suit.

—K—

KEY CARD BLACKWOOD
See FIVE ACE BLACKWOOD, ROMAN KEY-CARD BLACKWOOD

KIBITZER
An onlooker at bridge, or other games.

KILL
To remove the entries to a hand and thus render it worthless.

KISS
Acronym for 'Keep It Simple, Stupid'.

KISS OF DEATH
A penalty of 200 points at duplicate, usually a disastrous result almost certainly being worse than any partscore that could be made by the opposition.

KITCHEN BRIDGE
Social bridge played using very basic, natural bidding methods.

KNAVE
The original name for the fourth-highest ranking card in a suit. It is now more usually called the Jack in order to avoid confusion with the King when hands are recorded.

KNOCK
1 At rubber bridge, an alternative to 'Pass'.
2 See ALERT

KNOCK OUT
To force an opponent to play a master card (e.g. 'To knock out the Ace').

KNOCK-OUT TOURNAMENT
Head-to-head teams of four competition with the losers being eliminated.

KOCH-WERNER REDOUBLE
An SOS redouble named after its Swedish inventors, which asks partner to choose another suit when the opponents have doubled. See SOS REDOUBLE

—L—

LANDY
A conventional defence to a 1NT opener whereby 2♣ shows at least 5–4 in the majors, in response to which the only artificial bid is 2◊, asking for the longer major. See DEFENCE TO 1NT

LATE PAIR
Various duplicate movements make provision for a pair arriving after the start of a session, but its admission is at the discretion of the Director.

LATE PLAY
Completion of a board not played during the allotted time.

LAVINTHAL
See McKENNEY

LAWS AND ETHICS COMMITTEE (OF THE EBU)
The Committee of the English Bridge Union established in

accordance with the Union's Constitution to be responsible for licensing arrangements for systems and conventions, and to deal with all matters concerned with the Laws and Ethics of duplicate bridge in England. See ENGLISH BRIDGE UNION, LAWS OF DUPLICATE CONTRACT BRIDGE

LAWS OF CONTRACT BRIDGE
The international code last revised in 1993 in accordance with which rubber bridge is played. The Laws are promulgated jointly by The Portland Club, The European Bridge League, The American Contract Bridge League and The World Bridge Federation.

LAWS OF DUPLICATE CONTRACT BRIDGE
The international code under which duplicate bridge is played. They are promulgated by the World Bridge Federation in association with the same bodies as the Laws of Contract Bridge. The latest revision was published in 1987 (in Britain by the English Bridge Union in conjunction with The Portland Club).

LAW OF TOTAL TRICKS
A theory which asserts that the number of tricks available to both sides if they play in their best fit is equal to the total number of trumps in both sides' best trump fit. For example if North–South have a nine-card heart fit and on best play and against best defence can make ten tricks, and East–West have an eight-card diamond fit, then East–West will be able to take seven tricks.

LAYDOWN
Term for a contract that is so certain that declarer could claim after the initial lead.

LEAD
The initial card played to a trick.

LEAD-DIRECTING BID
A bid made with the intention of suggesting an initial lead in that suit.

LEAD-DIRECTING DOUBLE
A double of a conventional or cue bid to suggest a lead of that suit.

LEAD-INHIBITING BIDS
A bid of a suit not held in strength, in the hope that the opposition is discouraged from leading the suit.

LEAD OUT OF TURN
A lead from the wrong hand. The Laws apply.

LEAD THROUGH
A player who leads to a trick is said to lead through the player on his left.

LEAD THROUGH STRENGTH
In general, a player sitting in front of dummy and unsure which suit to lead, should lead through dummy's stronger holding, in the hope or knowledge of leading up to partner's honours in the suit. For example (with North as the dummy):

```
                ♠ A Q 2
                ♡ 8 5 2
                  ┌─────────┐
      ♠ 7 4 3     │    N    │
      ♡ 7 4 3     │  W   E  │
                  │    S    │
                  └─────────┘
```

West, on lead with no definitive information to guide him, should lead a spade.

LEAD UP TO WEAKNESS
In general, a player sitting over dummy, and unsure which suit to lead, should lead up to dummy's weakness in the hope or knowledge of leading up to partner's honours in the suit. For example (with North as the dummy):

♠ A Q 2
♡ 8 5 2

♠ 7 4 3
♡ 7 4 3

East, on lead with no definitive information to guide him, should lead a heart.

LEADING FROM HONOURS
The standard leads from honour combinations are:
> Ace from A K (but King from A K doubleton)
> The higher of two touching honours
> Top of a doubleton
> Low (e.g. fourth highest) from other combinations

Notes:
1 Some players prefer to lead the King from A K.
2 Against a suit contract it is usual not to underlead an Ace.
3 Against a No Trump contract the lead of an honour usually guarantees the possession of at least three honour cards unless the lead is from a short suit. From a long suit headed by just two (touching) honours, the standard lead is a low card (e.g. fourth highest).

See JOURNALIST LEADS, ROMAN LEADS, STRONG KINGS AND TENS

LEAP
A jump bid often used to describe a jump to the probable final contract inviting partner to pass at his first opportunity.

LEAVE IN
To pass and, especially, to pass a penalty double by partner.

LEBENSOHL CONVENTION
A convention to improve definition when partner opens 1NT and the next player overcalls in a suit at the two-level. The basis of the convention is the use of a bid of 2NT as a conventional transfer

requiring opener to bid 3♣. This then creates an extra echelon of bids – direct bids, and bids after the Lebensohl 2NT. One sequence is used to show game-going values (traditionally the direct bid) whilst the other is employed on competitive hands (or invitationally if a competitive bid in the suit was available at the two-level). A double may be used as a traditional penalty double, or to show a raise to 2NT. For example if your partner's 1NT opening is overcalled with 2♡ then:

2♠	Competitive
3♠	Game-forcing
2NT	(3♣) 3♠ invitational
3◇	Game-forcing
2NT	(3♣) 3◇ competitive

LEG
Colloquial term for a game in a rubber.

LENGTH
The number of cards held in a particular suit.

LENGTH SIGNALS
See COUNT SIGNALS

LEVEL
The number of tricks above the book named in the bidding. See BOOK

LHO
Abbreviation for **L**eft-**H**and **O**pponent.

LIFT
Term meaning 'Raise'.

LIGHT
1 To be light means to go down in a contract.
2 To bid light means to bid with values below the acceptable range.
See RULE OF NINETEEN

LIGHTNER DOUBLE
A double of a freely-bid slam by the player not on lead to the first trick and which calls for an unusual lead. The suit called for is normally the first bid side suit of the hand which is about to become the dummy and often shows a void in the suit.

LIMIT BID
A bid which defines a player's hand accurately in terms of both strength and distribution, for example an opening of 1NT, or the 2♠ bid in the sequence: 1♠–NB–2♠.

LIMIT RAISE
A raise of partner's suit to an appropriate level on the assumption that partner has the lower range of values for his bid. It is not forcing.

LIMIT RESPONSE
A response which defines the strength of the responder's hand, e.g. 1♠–NB–3NT.

LINE
1 The horizontal line dividing a rubber bridge score sheet, hence the expressions 'Above the line' relating to penalties, overtricks and bonuses, and 'Below the line' for tricks bid and made.
2 The plan of play (as in 'The best line of play').
3 When (typically) four card suits are bid in ascending order they are said to be bid 'Up the line'.

LITTLE SLAM
See SMALL SLAM

LMX
A conventional defence to an opening three bid whereby a bid in the lower minor (LM) is used as a take-out request immediately after the opening bid and a double (X) is used in the fourth seat.

LOCAL POINTS
Points issued by the English Bridge Union and affiliated bodies

such as clubs and County Associations for success in tournaments. 100 Local Points are equivalent to one Master Point. See GREEN POINTS, MASTER POINTS, RANK, RANKING SYSTEMS, RED POINTS

LOCKED (IN OR OUT OF HAND)
To be unable to get the lead in or out of dummy or declarer's hand without loss.

LONG CARDS
Cards left in a suit when all other cards in the suit have been played.

LONG HAND
The hand with the greater length in a particular suit, especially the trump suit.

LONG SUIT
A suit with four or more cards in the same hand.

LOOSE DIAMOND
See PHONEY DIAMOND

LOSE THE LEAD
The gaining of the lead by an opponent, whether by design, by force, or by accident.

LOSER
A card which will lose a trick if it is led or played in following suit.

LOSER ON LOSER
To discard one losing card on another, as illustrated in the following examples:

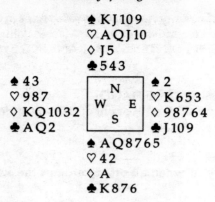

South plays in 4♠ and receives the lead of the ◊K. If East obtains the lead with the ♡K there is the danger of three club losers in addition to a heart loser. Therefore, after drawing trumps, declarer plays dummy's ◊J (West from his lead is presumed to hold the ◊Q) and discards a losing heart. He can then establish heart tricks by taking a ruffing finesse into the safe hand.

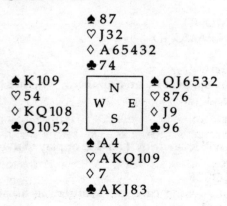

Playing in 6♡, South receives the lead of the ◊K. If he tries to ruff a club low, he will be overruffed and will subsequently lose a spade. He can however ruff a club once with the Jack and then return to hand with a spade to play another club; but this time, instead of ruffing, he makes the loser on loser play of discarding a spade from dummy. Dummy's hand can then ruff a losing spade in safety.

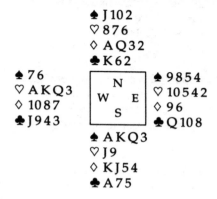

```
                    ♠ J 10 2
                    ♡ 876
                    ◊ A Q 3 2
                    ♣ K 6 2
    ♠ 76          ┌──────────┐    ♠ 9854
    ♡ A K Q 3     │    N     │    ♡ 10542
    ◊ 1087        │  W   E   │    ◊ 96
    ♣ J 9 4 3     │    S     │    ♣ Q 10 8
                  └──────────┘
                    ♠ A K Q 3
                    ♡ J 9
                    ◊ K J 5 4
                    ♣ A 7 5
```

South plays in 4♠ and three rounds of top hearts are led. If declarer ruffs the third round he will lose control of the trump suit on the probable 4–2 break. He should therefore discard a loser in clubs on the third round and dummy's trump holding is able to take care of any continuation in the suit.

There are many other variations when the loser on loser play is good declarer technique.

LOSING TRICK COUNT

A method of evaluating the playing strength of a hand, for trump contracts, based on the number of expected losers. The number of losers is determined as follows: With three or more cards, the number of losers in a suit is equal to the number of missing high honours (the Ace, King and Queen) e.g. A x x counts as two losers, K Q x or K Q x x count as one loser. With a doubleton, the Queen is counted as a small card in the above calculation, and similarly with any singleton, other than the Ace, the suit counts as one loser. The maximum number of losers a hand may have is thus twelve, and the most the two combined hands could have is twenty-four. So a six-loser hand opposite an eight-loser hand would have fourteen losers between the two and therefore they should make ten tricks. Subtract the combined number of losers from the total possible number of losers and the result equates to the number of tricks which should be available (i.e. 24–14=10). The main advantage of the Losing Trick Count over the Milton Work Count is that the Losing Trick Count is more accurate with good trump fits. See MILTON WORK COUNT

LOVE ALL
Neither side vulnerable. Both sides non-vulnerable.

LOVE SCORE
Neither side vulnerable and, in rubber bridge, no partscore.

LOW CARD
Any card other than an honour card and denoted by an 'x' on hand records.

LOW REVERSE
A rebid by opener in a higher-ranking new suit at the two-level. This bid is normally forcing for one round. For example: 1♣–NB–1♡–NB–2◊.

LOWER MINOR
A conventional defence to an opening three-bid. Using this convention, a bid of the lower unbid minor (3◊ over 3♣ or 4♣ over anything else) is a take out request. The advantage of this defence is that all other suit overcalls, 3NT and a double can be used in their natural sense. See DEFENCE TO OPENING THREE BID

—M—

McKENNEY
A system of signals and discards to show suit preference. The McKenney signal is made in two main defensive situations, normally against trump contracts:

1. On partner's opening lead of an Ace, when it is obvious from the bidding and sight of dummy, that a switch is called for at Trick Two. The play of a high card in the suit under the Ace calls for

the higher-ranking of the other two suits, excluding the trump suit; and a low card calls for the lower-ranking of the other two suits.

2. On the opening lead of a singleton to partner's Ace. When partner returns the suit for a ruff, he plays a significantly high or low card to indicate the suit of a second entry to his hand, in order to achieve a second ruff.

The McKenney discard works on the similar principle, except that it is normally used against No Trumps and occurs at a later stage of the defence. A low card asks for the lower of the two remaining suits, other than the suit of the discard; a high card asks for the higher of the other two suits. See SUIT PREFERENCE SIGNAL

MAJOR PENALTY CARD
See PENALTY CARD

MAJOR SUITS
Hearts and spades, often called 'the majors'. See MINOR SUITS

MAJOR TENACE
The holding of the highest and third-highest cards in a suit (A–Q). This combination will always yield one trick and, if the missing card lies in front of the tenace or the opponent with the missing card can be forced to open up the suit, two tricks can be made. See MINOR TENACE, TENACE

MAKE
1 To shuffle the deck.
2 To make enough tricks for the contract.
3 To win a trick.

MAKE UP A TABLE
For a fourth player to join with three others to play a game of bridge.

MANNERISM
A peculiarity of action or behviour (such as scratching one's ear)

which should be carefully avoided at the bridge table. Most unethical mannerisms are unconscious and not known by the player himself.

MARKED CARD
A card that is known to be in a particular hand.

MARKED FINESSE
A finesse when one opponent is marked with the missing card.

MASTER
1 An expert player.
2 A player who has won 50 Master Points. See RANKING SYSTEM

MASTER CARD
The highest outstanding card in a suit.

MASTER HAND
The hand with control of the trump suit.

MASTER PAIRS
An event, usually by invitation, for players of the highest standard.

MASTER POINTS
Points issued by the English Bridge Union and affiliated bodies such as clubs and County Associations for success in certain tournaments. There are two types of Master Point, Local and National. Local Points are awarded in all tournaments including club duplicates. National Points are awarded only in certain major tournaments. The accumulation of Master Points is necessary to attain the various grades in the EBU's ranking system. See GREEN POINTS, LOCAL POINTS, RANK, RANKING SYSTEMS, RED POINTS

MATCH PLAY
Head-to-head competition. See POINT-A-BOARD

MATCHPOINT(S)
In a duplicate pairs event, the result of the conversion of a pair's absolute score on any board to a ranking score. Two matchpoints are awarded for every pair beaten and one for every pair with the same score. To 'matchpoint' is to do this conversion. In a teams event, to matchpoint is to convert the aggregate difference on any board into IMPs.

MEAN SCORE
A score computed for a board at duplicate play, for which IMP's can be determined. See INTERNATIONAL MATCH POINTS

MENACE
A word primarily used in the context of Squeeze Play. See THREAT CARD (MENACE)

MERRIMAC COUP
The sacrifice of an honour, usually a King, as an entry killing manoeuvre. For example:

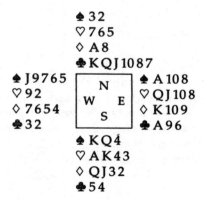

```
              ♠ 32
              ♡ 765
              ◊ A8
              ♣ K Q J 10 8 7
♠ J 9 7 6 5   ┌─────────┐   ♠ A 10 8
♡ 92          │    N    │   ♡ Q J 10 8
◊ 7654        │  W   E  │   ◊ K 10 9
♣ 32          │    S    │   ♣ A 9 6
              └─────────┘
              ♠ K Q 4
              ♡ A K 4 3
              ◊ Q J 3 2
              ♣ 54
```

Against 3NT, West leads ♣6 and East wins with the Ace. He then plays ◊K to force out dummy's Ace. Although this play gives up a trick, it prevents declarer from establishing dummy's club winners.

MICHAELS CUE BID
The use of the simple cue bid, i.e. a direct overcall in the suit opened by an opponent (as in the sequence 1♣–2♣ or 1♠–2♠), to show a two-suited hand. The cue bid of a minor shows the majors and the cue bid of a major shows the other major and a minor suit, after which 2NT is an enquiry as to which minor suit is held. The original convention admitted hands with 5–4 shape but the modern style demands at least 5–5.

MILTON WORK COUNT
The 4–3–2–1 honour point count used by most players. It was invented by Milton Work and was based on the McCampbell count of 1915. See HIGH CARD POINTS

MINI NO TRUMP
An opening 1NT bid showing 10–12 high card points.

MINOR PENALTY CARD
See PENALTY CARD

MINOR SUITS
Clubs and diamonds, often called 'the minors'. See MAJOR SUITS

MINOR SUIT SWISS
A convention whereby responses of 3♡ and 3♠ (and optionally 3◇ after 1♣) to an opening of one of a minor show good trump support, sound values for at least 3NT and some slam interest. The convention has the advantage that responder can show his support and values without taking the bidding beyond 3NT. The Swiss response may be used either to show a strong holding in the suit bid or to show specific hand-types. See SWISS CONVENTION

MINOR TENACE
A holding of the second and fourth highest cards in a suit i.e. K J. See MAJOR TENACE, TENACE

MIRROR DISTRIBUTION
See DUPLICATION OF DISTRIBUTION

MISBOARDING
Term used when the hands are replaced in the wrong slots in the board at duplicate play. If this means that the next table is unable to play the board, then the guilty pair or pairs will usually be fined.

MISDEAL
A misdeal occurs if a card is faced during the deal, or any player receives the incorrect number of cards.

MISERE
A player is said to have followed a misère (slang) line if his play was inferior, especially very inferior. 'Butcher' and 'Carve' are similar terms.

MISFIT
Description of a situation when both hands of a partnership contain two long suits but no fit.

MITCHELL MOVEMENT
A simple pairs movement in which the N–S pairs remain stationary, the E–W pairs move to the next higher table and the boards to the next lower table after each round. If there is an even number of tables then the middle round is a 'skip' round, with boards moving as normal but E–W pairs moving up two tables. Alternatively a 'relay' movement is used with the first and last tables sharing boards and a relay set of boards between the middle tables.

MIXED PAIRS
A competition in which each pair comprises a man and a woman. See FLITCH

MODIFIED GRAND SLAM FORCE
After the trump suit has been agreed, a bid of 5NT, bypassing 4NT, enquires about the Grand Slam. There are various

modifications of the convention, but the most common are:
1 6♣ – shows none of the top three honours
   6 of the agreed suit shows one of the top three honours
2 6♣ – shows one of the top three honours
   6 of the agreed suit shows none of the top honours

With two of the top honours, in both cases responder bids the Grand Slam. See GRAND SLAM FORCE

MONSTER
A very powerful hand.

MORTON'S FORK COUP
A term used to describe a play when, like the victims of Henry VII's Lord Chancellor, Cardinal Morton, whatever the defender's answer, it is wrong. Here is an example:

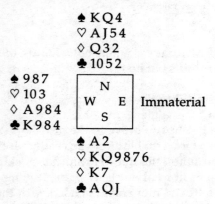

```
                    ♠ K Q 4
                    ♡ A J 5 4
                    ◇ Q 3 2
                    ♣ 1 0 5 2
        ♠ 9 8 7     ┌─────────┐
        ♡ 1 0 3     │    N    │
        ◇ A 9 8 4   │ W     E │  Immaterial
        ♣ K 9 8 4   │    S    │
                    └─────────┘
                    ♠ A 2
                    ♡ K Q 9 8 7 6
                    ◇ K 7
                    ♣ A Q J
```

Playing in a contract of 6♡, South receives a trump lead and potentially may lose a diamond and a club. However if he plays a small diamond from hand towards dummy's Q 3 2, West has no recourse. If he rises with the Ace then dummy's Queen will be established for a second club discard (the spade suit taking care of one losing club). If West ducks, declarer is able to discard the King from his hand on a spade and just loses one club.

MOVE
The change of seats by certain players in a duplicate pairs or teams event at the end of each round.

MOVEMENT
A schedule determining the movement at the end of each round.
See HOWELL, MITCHELL

MOVEMENT CARDS
Cards placed on each table in a duplicate event directing players to their next table at the end of each round.

MOYSIAN FIT
A 4–3 trump fit is said to be a Moysian fit. The term is named after Alphonse Moyse Jnr, whose bidding style often resulted in his trump contracts being played with only a 4–3 fit.

MUD
Standing for **M**iddle-**U**p-**D**own, this is a method of leading from a three-card suit (with no honour holding in the suit) by leading the middle card and on the next play of the suit following with the highest card. Partner is therefore able to identify that the suit is not a doubleton.

MULTI
See MULTICOLOURED TWO DIAMOND OPENER

MULTICOLOURED TWO DIAMOND OPENER
A conventional 2◊ opening bid used to show three or four distinctly different types of hand, including at least one weak and one strong type. The most popular version of the convention shows either a weak two-bid in a major, or a strong two bid in a minor or a strong balanced hand. Other strong options are a minor two-suited hand and an unspecified three-suited hand (4–4–4–1 or 5–4–4–0). See DEFENCE TO MULTI, DIXON

—N—

NATURAL
A suit bid which guarantees some holding in the suit named, or a No Trump bid suggesting the hand is playable in no trumps.

NEGATIVE DOUBLE
A double after partner has opened the bidding and right-hand opponent intervenes with a suit call, to show values and usually four cards in an unbid major. It is for take-out, not penalties. It is also called a Sputnik double, because it was first introduced in the same year as the Russian spacecraft, 1957.

NEGATIVE INFERENCE
An inference about the lie of the cards drawn by considering why an opponent did not choose an alternative bid or play.

NEGATIVE RESPONSE
A response denying values, often after a strong artificial opening. See DENIAL BID, HERBERT NEGATIVE

NEUTRAL CARD
A card played which gives no signal or inference about the strength or distribution of the suit.

NEUTRAL LEAD
See PASSIVE LEAD

NEXT STEP FOR KINGS
An agreement whereby, after the response to an Ace-asking 4♣ or 4NT, a bid of the next step, provided it is not the agreed trump suit, asks for Kings. See ROLLING BLACKWOOD, ROLLING GERBER

NIBU
See Northern Ireland Bridge Union.

NO BID
Term signifying 'Pass'. Traditional in Britain.

NO TRUMP
Highest-ranking denomination at bridge.

NO TRUMP FOR TAKE-OUT
A defence to weak three openings whereby an overcall of 3NT is used as a take-out request allowing all other calls to be natural, including a penalty double. See DEFENCE TO OPENING THREE BID

NON-FORCING
A bid which does not demand a response from partner.

NON-FORCING SEQUENCE
Any sequence of bidding, which is not forcing, such as the following examples:

1 1♡–1♠–2♡
2 1♡–1♠–2♡–3♣–3♡
3 1♡–2♣–2◇–2♡
4 1♡–2♣–2◇–3◇

NON-PLAYING CAPTAIN (NPC)
Most international teams of major bridge-playing countries now appoint captains who are not a playing member of the team. The main responsibility is to decide who plays in various stages of the contest, and the tactics to be followed. He or she also represents the team in discussions about playing conditions, protests and appeals, and at social events, press conferences, etc.

NON-VULNERABLE (NOT VULNERABLE)
The condition of a side that has not yet won a game. See GREEN, WHITE

NORMAN 4NT
A slam convention in which Aces and Kings are shown with one bid. An Ace is counted as one point and a King as a ½ point.

Responses are made on the following scale:

5♣ less than 1 ½ points
5◇ 1 ½ points (one Ace and one King, or three Kings)
5♡ 2 points (two Aces, four Kings, or one Ace and two Kings)
5♠ 2 ½ points (two Aces and one King, or one Ace and three Kings)
5NT 3 points, etc

NORTH
One of the compass positions at the bridge table. In duplicate, North has the responsibility for scoring the hand and overseeing the boards at the table.

NORTHERN IRELAND BRIDGE UNION
Regulatory body for Duplicate Bridge in Northern Ireland.

NOTTINGHAM CLUB SYSTEM
A simple English 1♣ system popular in the Nottingham area. The system is based on an artificial 1♣ opening (16–21 points) and five-card majors.

NUISANCE BID
A bid aiming to disrupt the opposition's auction.

—O—

OBLIGATORY FINESSE
The play of a small card on the second round of a suit in the hope that a particular opponent will have to play the master card. For example:

```
            K432
          ┌───────┐
          │   N   │
    A8    │ W   E │  J109
          │   S   │
          └───────┘
            Q765
```

The only way to avoid two losers in the suit is for South, declarer, to play a small card towards dummy and, after winning the King, play small from both hands. If the East-West hands were reversed, it would be necessary to play initially from the North hand towards South's Q 7 6 5.

ODD-EVEN DISCARDS
A system of discards in which the face value (odd/even) of the discard is used to signal count, attitude, or suit preference.

ODD TRICK
Each trick won by declarer in excess of the book. 'One odd' is one trick in excess (i.e. declarer's seventh trick). See BOOK

OFFENCE
1 Any breach of the Law.
2 Attacking mode in bidding or play.

OFFSIDE
When a finesse is wrong, the missing card is said to be 'offside'. See FINESSE, ONSIDE

OLYMPIAD
See WORLD CHAMPIONSHIPS

ONE-BID
A bid at the one-level.

ONE CLUB SYSTEM
A system of bidding which employs an artificial bid of 1♣ as its strongest opening. Usually the bid denotes a minimum of about 16 or 17 points. See BLUE CLUB, PRECISION, ROMAN SYSTEM

ONE OVER ONE RESPONSE
A sequence such as 1♣–1♡, where responder bids at the one-level.

ONE-SUITER
An unbalanced hand with one long suit and no other suit of more than three cards.

ONSIDE
If a finesse works,the missing card is said to be 'onside'. See FINESSE, OFFSIDE

OPEN
1 To make the first bid in the auction.
2 Teams or pairs competition where no restriction applies to the contestants (sex, age, master point ranking, etc.).

OPEN HAND
Dummy.

OPEN PAIRS
Competition open to anyone, irrespective of membership, age, master point ranking or sex. In British congresses, where entry to the main event is restricted, it is customary for an Open Pairs event to be run simultaneously.

OPEN ROOM
Room where spectators are allowed in a teams competition.

OPEN UP
To 'open up' a suit is to play the first cards in that suit.

OPENING BID
The first call of the auction other than pass.

OPENING LEAD
The initial lead to the first trick, before the dummy is seen.

OPTIONAL DOUBLE
A double suggesting all-round strength and inviting partner to choose between bidding on or defending for penalties.

ORANGE BOOK
Colloquial term for *The Handbook of Directives and Conventions Authorized by The Laws and Ethics Committee of The English Bridge Union.*

OUT-OF-THE-BLUE CUE BID
See ADVANCE CUE BID

OUT ON A LIMB
Phrase used to describe a dangerous action such as bidding No Trumps with no stop in an opponent's suit.

OVER
Term describing a player's hand with respect to his right-hand opponent, e.g. 'Sitting over'.

OVERBID
1 Old term for an overcall.
2 A call made on insufficient values.

OVERBIDDER
A person who overbids.

OVERBOARD
To be at too high a level.

OVERCALL
1 The first bid by a member of the side that did not open the bidding.
2 To make such a bid.

OVERRUFF
To ruff a trick, which has already been ruffed, with a higher trump.

OVERTAKE
To play a higher card from one hand when already winning a trick. Often used when a hand is devoid of entries and the suit is blocked.

OVERTRICK
A trick in excess of the number contracted for. Overtricks do not count towards game and, in rubber bridge, are scored above the line.

OVERTRUMP
See OVERRUFF

—P—

PACK
The deck of 52 playing cards.

PAIR
A partnership of two bridge players.

PAIRS EVENT
An event in which players compete as pairs, normally with matchpoint scoring.

PALOOKA
A very poor bridge player.

PAR
The result on a board if both sides had bid and played to the optimum result.

PAR CONTEST
A contest, usually using preset hands of great technical difficulty, where players are rewarded for achieving or beating the par result on each board instead of the actual result. Aggregate, matchpoint and International Match Point scoring can all be used.

PARTIAL
See PARTSCORE

PARTIAL DESIGNATION
An incomplete request for a card to be played from dummy. If the suit alone is named, the lowest card in the suit must be played. If the rank of the card alone is named, the card must, if there is ambiguity, be taken from the last suit led.

PARTIAL ELIMINATION
A play by which a declarer only partially eliminates the suits which a defender may safely lead when he is thrown in. Whether the defender will have to lead to declarer's advantage depends on distributional factors.

PARTNER
One of the two members of a partnership.

PARTNERSHIP RUBBER BRIDGE
Rubber bridge where players retain the same partner throughout the session of play.

PARTNERSHIP UNDERSTANDING
An agreement between members of a partnership regarding conventions in bidding and play, allowing for more efficient communication. Such agreements, whether explicit or implicit, must be fully and freely available to opponents.

PARTSCORE
A trick score of less than 100 points. It is also known as a 'partial'.

PARTSCORE, BIDDING TO THE
Bidding affected by the presence of a partscore.

PARTSCORE BONUS
See BONUS

PASS
Call by which a player indicates that he does not wish, or is not allowed by the Laws, to enter the bidding at his turn to bid. See NO BID

PASS-OUT
1 A hand is said to be 'passed-out' if all four players pass without any player having bid. At rubber bridge, the deal passes to the next player, at Chicago the same player must redeal, and at duplicate bridge the hands are replaced in the board as if

played and the score recorded as no score to either side.
2 To make the third consecutive pass after the bidding has been opened.

PASS OUT OF TURN
A 'Pass' by a player when it is not his turn to call. The Laws apply.

PASS-OUT SEAT
A player is said to be in the pass-out seat if the auction would end if he passed.

PASSED HAND
A hand which has already passed (and therefore, if its holder subsequently makes a bid, that bid is limited in value by his previous pass).

PASSIVE DEFENCE
A style of defence which attempts to avoid establishing tricks for declarer as opposed to actively trying to establish tricks for the defenders.

PASSIVE LEAD
A lead made more in an attempt to avoid conceding a trick than to establish one. See ATTACKING LEAD

PATTERN
See HAND PATTERN

PENALTY
1 A score arising from the failure to make a contract.
2 The sanction imposed by the Laws, or by the Tournament Director, for an irregularity or an infraction.

PENALTY CARD
A card that is wrongly played or exposed may become a penalty card. In duplicate some penalty cards are designated 'minor' penalty cards, others 'major' penalty cards. In rubber there is no such distinction. The Laws apply.

PENALTY DOUBLE
A double made in the belief that the opposing contract will not make. It is also known as a 'Business double'.

PENALTY PASS
To pass a non-penalty double thus effectively converting it to a penalty double.

PERCENTAGE PLAY
The line most likely to succeed based on mathematical probabilities. See PROBABILITIES OF DISTRIBUTION

PERMUTATION
Term describing all possible arrangements of a set of objects and, in bridge, the possible disposition of the cards.

PERSONAL SCORE CARD
The card on which a player may record all the details of his bridge session, including the outline of his bidding system and conventions, as well as contracts played and results achieved on each board of the session.

PETER
The play by a defender of a high card on the first round of a suit followed by a lower card on the second round to signal to partner. Usually the peter is used to show that the signaller likes the suit or that he has an even number of cards in it. The peter is also known as an 'echo' or 'high-low' signal. See REVERSE PETER

PHANTOM PAIR
If the number of pairs at a duplicate event is not even, there will be a table with only one pair (a half table). In consequence, on every round one pair will be due to play the 'phantom pair' and will instead spend that round sitting out.

PHANTOM SACRIFICE
A sacrifice bid when the contract against which one is sacrificing could not be made. See SACRIFICE

PHONEY CLUB
A rudimentary system based on a strong No Trump and five-card suit openings in diamonds, hearts and spades, with a (possibly) phoney club being the first move on other hands. 'Fishing Club', 'Short Club' and 'Utility Club' are similar systems.

PHONEY DIAMOND
An opening of 1◊ used in much the same way as a phoney 1♣. It is also known as a 'Loose Diamond'.

PICK UP
To win a certain number of tricks, or to capture a particular card (e.g. 'To play a small spade to hand picking up the Queen').

PICK UP SLIP
Used in place of a traveller and collected by a caddy during a competition. See CADDY, TRAVELLER OR TRAVELLING SCORESLIP

PIN

```
            A 10987
              ┌───────┐
              │   N   │
        K 65  │ W   E │  J
              │   S   │
              └───────┘
             Q 432
```

The lead of the Queen towards the Ace brings in five tricks when, as here, the Jack is singleton and on the right and therefore 'pinned' by the Queen.

PIP
A design on the front of the playing card showing the card's rank by the number of pips, and the suit by the shape of the pip. Different pips are used in different countries, hearts, cloves, acorns, leaves etc.

PITCH
To discard.

PIVOT TEAMS
A teams contest whereby members of each team change partnerships so that by the end of the contest every member of each team has played a proportion of the boards with every other member of the team as a partner.

PLACING THE CARDS
The diagnosis of the position of key cards from clues arising from the bidding or play.

PLAN OF PLAY
The mental process which declarers should follow in determining their best line of play to make their contracts.

PLAY
1 The play follows the auction.
2 Used to describe an action in the play, e.g. 'The key play is to ruff a diamond'.

PLAY OUT OF TURN
The play of a card when it is not one's turn to play. The Laws apply.

PLAYED CARD
A defender plays a card by placing it face up on the table in front of him. If a defender places a card in such a position that the other defender can see the front of the card, it is deemed to have been played. Declarer plays a card in a similar manner and any card placed face up, on or near the surface of the table, by declarer is deemed to have been played. Declarer plays dummy's cards by either naming them (the correct procedure in duplicate bridge) or physically handling them (in rubber bridge).

PLAYER
One of the four people who participate in a game of bridge.

PLAYING A KNOWN CARD

If a player has the choice between cards, it is sometimes better to play the one which he is known to hold. For example:

```
              A J 4
            ┌───────┐
            │   N   │
    Q 10 8  │ W   E │  5 3 2
            │   S   │
            └───────┘
              K 9 7 6
```

South, declarer, plays a small card and successfully finesses the Jack. When the Ace is played West should drop the Queen (the card he is known to hold) presenting South with a choice of plays, finessing East for the 10 or playing for the even break. If West follows with the 10 on the second round declarer will inevitably play for the break.

PLAYING CARDS

The set of fifty-two cards with which the game of bridge is played. The pack consists of four suits, clubs, diamonds, hearts and spades (ascending rank order) each containing thirteen cards: Ace, King, Queen, Jack, 10, 9, 8, 7, 6, 5, 4, 3, 2 (descending rank order), the rank indicated by a pictorial image and/or the number of pips, the suit indicated by the shape and colour of the pip.

PLAYING TO THE SCORE

To allow one's decisions regarding bidding or play to be influenced by the score. Typically, to underbid at rubber bridge with a partscore.

PLAYING-TRICK

A card which can reasonably be expected to win a trick given a normal distribution of the cards and ignoring the possibility of losing tricks to ruffs; e.g. A K Q x x x is six playing tricks and A K Q x x x x is seven.

PLUS VALUES

See HONOUR TRICKS

POCKET
Part of a duplicate wallet or board used to hold the cards.

PODI
Method of coping with intervention after partner's Blackwood bid. **P**ass shows zero (**O**) Aces. **D**ouble shows one (**I**) Ace and the lowest bid two etc. See DOPI/ROPI

POINT-A-BOARD
One scoring method of determining a winner in a teams-of-four match. Each board is taken individually, one point is scored for a win and half a point for a tie. In Britain it is more common to award two points for a win and one for a tie.

POINT COUNT
A method of hand valuation by points, the most popular of which is the Milton Work count: four for an Ace, three for a King, two for a Queen, one for a Jack. See DISTRIBUTIONAL POINT COUNT

POINTED SUITS
Diamonds and Spades, so called because of the shape of their symbols. Clubs and hearts are similarly called 'Rounded Suits'.

POKER BRIDGE
A style of bidding and play, which has an unduly large element of gambling about it.

PORI
After a 4NT Ace enquiry is doubled, **P**ass shows zero (**O**) Aces, and **R**edouble shows one (**I**).

PORTLAND CLUB, THE
First body to codify the Laws of Bridge (1895). Originally The Stratford Club, it was reorganized to remove an unpleasant member. It is still an important authority in the world of international bridge and holds the copyright to the Laws in many parts of the world.

PORTLAND RULES
Rules laid down by The Portland Club which included banning the use of any conventional bids in the club's cardrooms.

POSITION
1 The cardinal compass point (N–S–E–W) of a player.
2 A player's position in relation to the dealer (first hand is the dealer, second hand is on the dealer's left etc.), or in relation to another player; to sit over/behind (to be the left-hand opponent) or under/in front of (to be the right-hand opponent).

POSITIONAL FACTOR
The value of a particular holding may change as the auction develops, thus indicating the likely disposition of the other relevant cards. For instance a holding of K x in a suit is more valuable if the suit has been bid by the right-hand opponent rather than by the left-hand opponent. Thus the positional factor affects its value.

POSITIONAL SQUEEZE
A squeeze which is effective against one opponent but not the other, i.e. which will not operate if the opponents' hands are interchanged. See SQUEEZE

POSITIVE RESPONSE
A constructive response guaranteeing some conventionally agreed minimum strength.

POST MORTEM
The discussion of a bridge hand after it has been played.

POSTING THE SCORE
To place the overall results chart of an event where it is accessible to the competitors.

POWERHOUSE
A hand of tremendous trick-taking ability.

PRECISION
A bidding system that originated in Taiwan and was developed by C. C. Wei in the 1960s. It achieved world attention when the team from Nationalist China finished second in both the 1969 and 1970 World Championships. The system is based on an artificial 1♣ (16+ points) opening and five-card majors.

PRE-DEALING
The dealing of the hands in advance of the competition in which they are to be played. See SIMULTANEOUS PAIRS

PRE-EMPTIVE BID OR SHUT-OUT BID
A weak high-level bid based upon the playing strength contained in a long suit, with few outside values. The bid is purely obstructive in nature and can make opposing bidding extremely difficult. See RULE OF TWO AND THREE

PRE-EMPTIVE RAISE
A raise based on distributional rather than high-card values in an attempt to pre-empt the opponents,(rather than necessarily reach a makeable contract – e.g. 1♠–NB–4♠).

PREFERENCE
To prefer partner's first-bid suit after being offered a choice. For example in the sequence: 1♡–NB–2♣–NB–2♢–NB–2♡, responder has given preference for hearts over diamonds, although since opener's first suit will invariably be at least as long as his second, responder would show 'preference' for opener's first suit if his two holdings were of equal length. Responder would 'prefer' the second suit by passing or raising. See FALSE PREFERENCE

PREPARED CLUB
An opening bid of 1♣ made on a balanced hand with possibly only a three-card (or even two card) club suit to prepare for a No Trump rebid.

PREPARED HANDS
See PAR CONTEST, SIMULTANEOUS PAIRS

PREPARED MINOR SUITS
An opening bid of 1♣ or 1◊ made on a balanced hand with possibly only a three-card suit to prepare for a No Trump rebid.

PREPAREDNESS, THE PRINCIPLE OF
The principle whereby one selects an opening bid so that one always has a sound rebid over any possible response.

PRESSURE BID
A bid made at a high level due to the presence of interference bidding. For example after 1♠–3♣, responder may have to bid 3♠ with 7–8 points and some spade support, less than that required for an uncontested 3♠ bid. Such a bid is said to be a 'pressure bid'.

PRIMARY SUPPORT
Four-card support for an opening bid of one of a suit. See SECONDARY SUPPORT

PRINCIPLE OF RESTRICTED CHOICE
See RESTRICTED CHOICE

PROBABILITIES OF DISTRIBUTION
The mathematically expected distribution of the opposing cards.

Opponents hold	Division	Probability (to nearest percent)
8 cards	5–3	47%
	4–4	33%
	6–2	17%
	7–1	3%
7 cards	4–3	62%
	5–2	31%
	6–1	7%
6 cards	4–2	48%
	3–1	36%
	5–1	15%
	6–0	1%

Opponents hold	Division	Probability (to nearest percent)
5 cards	3–2	68%
	4–1	28%
	5–0	4%
4 cards	3–1	50%
	2–2	40%
	4–0	10%
3 cards	2–1	78%
	3–0	22%
2 cards	1–1	52%
	2–0	48%

PROFESSIONAL
A bridge professional is a person who makes his living from the game of bridge, though not necessarily as a player.

PROGRESSIVE BRIDGE
A form of social bridge with several tables in play. The winners on a round move up a table while the losers stay put (or vice versa).

PROGRESSIVE SQUEEZE
A triple squeeze in which an opponent, having released control of one suit, is then squeezed again in the remaining two suits. For example:

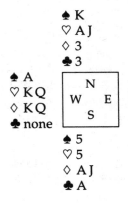

South plays the ♣A forcing West to relinquish control in one of the other three suits. South then cashes whichever suit West discards to squeeze him again in the other two suits. This type of squeeze can be positional, as here against West, or automatic.

PROMOTION
The play of one card to promote another to winning status. See TRUMP PROMOTION

PROPRIETIES
The rules of proper conduct, ethics and etiquette.

PROTECT
1 To have small cards with an honour in a suit e.g. a 'protected' King.
2 To bid after two successive passes in order that partner may have the opportunity to bid again. See BALANCING
3 To have a positional stopper. For example:

```
                K54
              ┌───────┐
              │   N   │
        QJ102 │ W   E │ A973
              │   S   │
              └───────┘
                86
```

North's King is protected from a lead by East, but not by West.

PROTECTION
See BALANCING

PROTEST PERIOD
The period of time in competitions, usually thirty minutes after the score has been posted, within which a player or players may request any anomaly in the scoring to be corrected or may register an appeal against a ruling by the Tournament Director.

PSEUDO SQUEEZE
A play which leads a defender to believe that a squeeze position exists when in fact none does. See SQUEEZE

PSYCHIC BID

A bid which deliberately and substantially mis-states the strength and/or distribution of a hand. See AMBER, GREEN, RED, SEMI-PSYCHIC BID

PUMP

Colloquialism for forcing declarer to ruff.

PUNCH

To force a player to shorten his trumps by ruffing.

PUNT

To bid directly to game or slam when more constructive and descriptive bids are available. The term normally refers to hands on which the player's game or slam bid is speculative rather than sound.

PUPPET STAYMAN

A version of Stayman for five-card and four-card suits following an opening bid of 1NT or 2NT. After 1NT–NB–2♣–NB–2◇ (denying a five-card major), responder bids the major in which he does not hold four cards. See STAYMAN CONVENTION

PUSH

1 To make an unconstructive raise in a competitive situation. The tactic is usually employed in the hope that the opponents will overbid.
2 A board in a teams match with zero swing (slang).

—Q—

QUANTITATIVE 4NT

The use of 4NT, usually as a direct raise of No Trumps, to request partner to pass or bid 6NT depending on whether he is minimum or maximum in the context of the previous bidding.

QUANTITATIVE 5NT
The use of 5NT, usually as a direct raise of No Trumps, to request partner to bid 6NT or 7NT depending on whether he is minimum or maximum in the context of the previous bidding.

QUEEN OVER JACK
An assumption, made in rubber bridge, that the Queen lies over the Jack more often than simple probabilities suggest. It is derived from the theory that in a previous hand the Queen may have covered the Jack and that, after the trick was gathered, the two had not been separated by the shuffle.

QUICK TRICK
See HONOUR TRICKS

QUITTED TRICK
In duplicate bridge a trick is quitted when all four players have turned their cards over. In rubber bridge a trick is quitted when the four cards making up the trick are gathered by the winning side. In duplicate a quitted trick may not be inspected although a player may look at, but not expose, his own card until a card is led to the next trick. In rubber, a player may inspect the previous trick until his side has played to the next trick.

—R—

RABBIT
An inexperienced player.

RACK
Apparatus to hold cards for handicapped players.

RAGS
A poor holding, e.g. 'two rags', a low doubleton.

RAISE
To increase the level of the contract in partner's last-mentioned denomination.

RANK
1 The relative value of the cards.
2 The status achieved in a ranking system.
3 The rank of the suits as used to distinguish between the major suits (spades and hearts) and the minor suits (diamonds and clubs).

RANKING SYSTEM
A system of measuring a player's ability and/or experience relative to other players. The English Bridge Union Ranking System is based on Master Points accumulated.

Rank	Master Points	
Club Master	2	
District Master	10	
County Master	25	
Master	50	
Advanced Master	75	
* Master	100	
** Master	150	
*** Master	200	
**** Master	250	
***** Master	300	
Tournament Master	400	
* Tournament Master	500	
** Tournament Master	600	
*** Tournament Master	700	
**** Tournament Master	800	
***** Tournament Master	900	
Regional Master	100	including 25 Green Points
Premier Regional Master	200	including 50 Green Points
National Master	300	including 75 Green Points
Premier National Master	400	including 100 Green Points
Life Master	600	including 150 Green Points
Premier Life Master	900	including 300 Green Points
Grand Master	1200	including 600 Green Points

Within the ranks of Regional and Premier Regional Master a star is prefixed for the attainment of each block of 100 Master Points in excess of 100 and 200 respectively. See GREEN POINTS, LOCAL POINTS, MASTER POINTS, RANK, RED POINTS

REBIDDABLE SUIT
A suit of five cards, normally headed by at least two of the top honours (Ace, King, Queen). Any six-card or longer suit.

RECAPITULATION SHEET
Sheet on which the results of each board, the totals for each pair and the final placings are posted after a duplicate event. See PROTEST PERIOD

RECTIFYING THE COUNT
The deliberate loss of a trick or tricks in preparation for a squeeze. For most squeezes to succeed, the squeeze card must be played when the declarer can take all the remaining tricks but one. If he has two tricks to lose then usually the squeeze will fail. However he can often remedy the situation by first removing a trick before playing the squeeze card. For example:

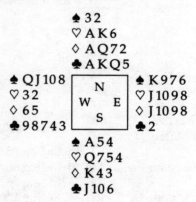

```
                    ♠ 32
                    ♡ A K 6
                    ◊ A Q 7 2
                    ♣ A K Q 5
      ♠ Q J 10 8    ┌─────────┐    ♠ K 9 7 6
      ♡ 32          │    N    │    ♡ J 10 9 8
      ◊ 65          │ W     E │    ◊ J 10 9 8
      ♣ 9 8 7 4 3   │    S    │    ♣ 2
                    └─────────┘
                    ♠ A 5 4
                    ♡ Q 7 5 4
                    ◊ K 4 3
                    ♣ J 10 6
```

South, playing in 6NT on the above hand, receives the lead of the ♠Q. Clearly the contract will be simple if either red suit divides 3–3. However South can also succeed if either opponent holds at least four cards in both red suits, for then he will be squeezed. If South wins the opening lead and then cashes four clubs only five tricks will have been played. Each player will have eight cards left and neither defender will have any difficulty in retaining four hearts and four diamonds, and so will not be squeezed. However if South ducks the opening lead, wins the spade continuation and then cashes four clubs, six tricks will have been played and only seven cards will remain in each hand. Thus neither defender will be able to retain four cards in both hearts and diamonds. Ducking the opening lead 'rectifies the count'.

RED

1 One of the traffic-light terms used by the Laws and Ethics Committee of the English Bridge Union to categorize psychic bids. A 'red' psyche is one where the partnership's subsequent actions provide sufficient evidence of an unauthorized partnership understanding to warrant an adjusted score. See AMBER, GREEN, PSYCHIC BID

2 Shorthand for describing the vulnerability of both partnerships on a board and meaning that the 'red' partnership is vulnerable but their opponents are not vulnerable. See AMBER, GREEN, WHITE

RED DOT

A marking to be placed on a convention card signifying that non-standard leads are being employed.

RED POINT

Scottish National Master Point, equivalent to an English Green Point. See GREEN POINT, LOCAL POINT, MASTER POINT RANK, RANKING SYSTEM

REDEAL

A second or subsequent deal following an irregularity during the original deal.

REDOUBLE

A call which doubles the value of tricks bid and made, the penalty for undertricks and the bonuses for overtricks of a contract which has already been doubled. It will also lead to an additional bonus ('for the insult') of 100 points if the contract is made. See SOS REDOUBLE

RE-ENTRY
A second entry.

REFUSE (TO WIN A TRICK)
See DUCK

RELAY
A bid, usually the cheapest bid, which does not convey any information but simply marks time while partner describes his hand. It is common in artificial systems.

RELAY SYSTEM
A bidding system which employs relays so that one member of the partnership describes his hand accurately and the other decides the final contract.

RELAY TABLE
Table used for boards not in play, particularly during a Howell movement or a relay Mitchell. See HOWELL, MITCHELL

REMOVE A DOUBLE
To bid again after partner has made a penalty double, thus signifying an unwillingness to defend the doubled contract.

RENEGE
Old fashioned term for revoke.

REOPEN THE BIDDING
A call made by a player who has initially passed and is sitting in the position that, were he to pass, the bidding would end. He may be acting in a balancing role. See BALANCING

REOPENING DOUBLE
A double, intended basically for take-out, used by the player in the pass-out seat to keep the auction alive. The call is often used by the

opener as an effective way of competing after partner has passed over an opponent's intervention, especially if negative doubles are part of the agreed system. See BALANCING

REPEATED FINESSE
To finesse more than once in the same suit against the same opponent. See DOUBLE FINESSE

REPECHAGE
A form of competition whereby competitors, knocked out in the qualifying stages of the main event, have a second opportunity to qualify for the final of the main event by winning a secondary event.

REPLAY DUPLICATE
A form of duplicate whereby two pairs play the same boards from both positions, popular in the 1920s in America.

RESCUE
To take out into what is hoped to be a safer contract.

RESERVE
To have an alternative line of play available, e.g. 'To keep the heart finesse in reserve'.

RESERVE ONE'S RIGHTS
To alert the opponents at the table that you believe an irregularity has occurred and therefore that you may need to call the Tournament Director.

RESPOND
To make a bid, usually after partner has opened the bidding but also if partner has made a take-out double or any other forcing bid.

RESPONDER
The player who responds.

RESPONDER'S REVERSE

A non-jump rebid by responder in a new suit which is higher-ranking than his first and is made at the two-level or above. For example:

Opener	Responder
1♣	1♡
2♣	2♠

A responder's reverse is normally played as forcing for one round.

RESPONSE

See RESPOND

RESPONSIVE DOUBLE

The use of a double for take-out when partner has already made a take-out double and the third player has supported the opener. For example:

Opener	Partner	Responder	You
1♣	Dble	3♣	Dble

The double suggests the values to compete but with no strong preference for a particular suit. Responsive doubles may be played to any level by partnership agreement. Up to and including 3♠ is a popular choice.

RESTRICTED CHOICE

The Principle of Restricted Choice is a mathematical principle based on the assumption that, with two cards of equal value, a player will play either of them randomly. For example:

$$
\text{A 3 2} \quad \boxed{\begin{array}{c} \text{N} \\ \text{W} \quad \text{E} \\ \text{S} \end{array}} \quad \text{K 10 9 8 7 6}
$$

West, declarer, plays the Ace and South (on his right) plays the Queen. Given that with Queen–Jack doubleton, South will half the time play the Jack and half the time play the Queen, East is twice as likely to hold the singleton Queen as he is the Queen–Jack doubleton.

RESTRICTED LICENCE
A treatment or convention licensed by the EBU for use only in certain competitions.

RESULTS MERCHANT
A player who extols the merits of a line of play, either because on the actual layout of the cards it would have succeeded, or because on the actual results on a board it would have scored well, rather than on sound, logical analysis.

RETAIN THE LEAD
To keep the lead by playing a card known to be a winner.

REVALUATION
The mental adjustment to the value of one's hand in the light of the previous bidding. For example a holding of K x is more likely to be useful if it is held in a suit bid by one's right-hand opponent rather than by one's left-hand opponent.

REVERSE
A non-jump rebid in a new suit by opener above the level of two of his original suit. See HIGH REVERSE, LOW REVERSE

REVERSE BENJAMIN
See BENJAMINISED ACOL (BENJAMIN CONVENTION)

REVERSE SIGNALS/DISCARDS
A method of signalling/discarding whereby a low card is encouraging and a high card is discouraging. This reverses the standard high-low signals/discards. The chief advantage is that, with a doubleton, a player does not need to use what may be an important card, which he cannot afford, to encourage.

REVERSING THE DUMMY
See DUMMY REVERSAL

REVIEWING THE BIDDING
A player may, at his turn to call, request a review of the auction.

At duplicate, such a review must be given by an opponent and must include every call, including alerts.

REVOKE
To fail to follow suit when able to do so. A revoke becomes established when either member of the offending side plays to the next trick. The Laws apply.

REVOLVING DISCARDS
A system of discards whereby the rank of the discard signals a suggested lead. Against No Trump contracts, a discard of a high card asks for the lead of the suit ranking immediately above the suit of the discard (clubs above spades) and similarly for a low ranking discard (spades before clubs). For example:

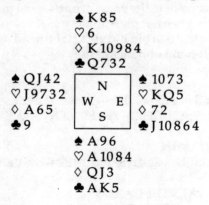

```
              ♠ K 8 5
              ♡ 6
              ◇ K 10 9 8 4
              ♣ Q 7 3 2
♠ QJ42      ┌─────────┐   ♠ 1073
♡ J9732     │    N    │   ♡ KQ5
◇ A65       │  W   E  │   ◇ 72
♣ 9         │    S    │   ♣ J10864
            └─────────┘
              ♠ A 9 6
              ♡ A 10 8 4
              ◇ QJ3
              ♣ AK5
```

South, playing in 3NT, receives the lead of the ♡3, East plays the Queen, taken by South's Ace. When South plays diamonds, West holds up his Ace until the third round to allow his partner the chance to signal. Playing 'revolving discards', on the third round of diamonds the ♠3 or the ♣J will ask for a heart continuation.

RHO
Abbreviation for **R**ight-**H**and **O**pponent.

RHYTHM
To bid or play in rhythm is to bid or play at an even speed. See TEMPO.

RIDE
To take a finesse by playing a card and letting it run, if not covered by LHO. For example:

$$QJ1032 \quad \boxed{\begin{array}{c} N \\ W \quad E \\ S \end{array}} \quad A75$$

West leads the Queen and lets it 'ride' unless North covers with the King.

RIFFLE SHUFFLE
An effective form of shuffling by allowing two portions of a pack to become interwoven in a fairly random manner. A perfect riffle shuffle (two portions perfectly interwoven) is thus not a true shuffle at all since a second identical shuffle restores the pack to its original form.

RIPSTRA
A defence to an opening 1NT bid whereby a 2♣ overcall shows both majors with longer clubs than diamonds and a 2◊ overcall shows both majors with longer diamonds than clubs. See DEFENCE TO 1NT

ROCK-CRUSHER
A hand of tremendous trick-taking ability.

ROLLING BLACKWOOD
After a Blackwood 4NT enquiry some players use the cheapest available (non-trump suit) bid to ask for Kings instead of using 5NT. This is called 'Rolling Blackwood' or 'Sliding Blackwood'.

ROLLING FOUR NO TRUMP
See GENERAL PURPOSE CUE BID

ROLLING GERBER

A convention whereby after the response to 4♣, a relay in the cheapest non-trump suit subsequently asks for Kings. It is also called Sliding Gerber. See GERBER

ROMAN ASKING BIDS

A method of establishing the suitability of the two hands for slam purposes. In certain situations, when a trump suit has been agreed, a bid of a new suit asks partner to describe his holding in that suit on the following scale:

1st step	No control
2nd step	King or singleton
3rd step	Ace or void
4th step	Ace-King or Ace-Queen

ROMAN BLACKWOOD

A version of Blackwood originally used in the Roman system. After 4NT, the responses are:

5♣ Shows zero or three Aces
5♢ Shows one or four Aces

The responses of 5♡, 5♠ and 5NT show two Aces, either of the same colour, the same rank or the two other Aces. The original school of thought was:

5♡ Shows two Aces of the same colour
5♠ Shows two Aces neither of which are the same rank nor the same colour (i.e. spades and diamonds or hears and clubs)
5NT Shows two Aces of the same rank

Some players prefer the CRO principle, i.e. 5♡ same **C**olour, 5♠ same **R**ank, 5NT the two **O**ther. A player can then ask for Kings in a similar way. See BLACKWOOD

ROMAN GERBER

A version of Gerber modelled on the same lines as Roman Blackwood. See GERBER, ROMAN BLACKWOOD

ROMAN JUMP OVERCALL

A system of two-suited jump overcalls whereby immediate jump suit overcalls show intermediate two-suiters, when the lower-ranking of two touching suits (excluding the opener's suit) is bid, whilst a 2NT overcall shows a strong unspecified two-suiter. See TWO-SUITED OVERCALLS

ROMAN KEY-CARD BLACKWOOD
A variation of Blackwood in which the King of the trump suit is treated as a 'fifth' Ace. The responses to 4NT are:

5♣ 0 or 3 Aces
5◊ 1 or 4 Aces
5♡ 2 or 5 Aces but not the Queen of trumps
5♠ 2 or 5 Aces including the Queen of trumps
5NT 2 Aces plus a useful void

After a 5♣ or 5◊ response, the 4NT bidder may continue with a bid in the lowest non-trump suit to enquire whether the Queen of trumps is held. The responder returns to the trump suit at the lowest level without the Queen and either bids 5NT or cue bids a second-round control with it. An alternative method is for responder to proceed: one step without the Queen, two steps with it.

The 4NT bidder can continue with a bid of 5NT to ask for the non-trump Kings. Responses are on the standard step principle:

6♣ 0 King
6◊ 1 King
6♡ 2 Kings
6♠ 3 Kings

ROMAN LEADS
A system of leads whereby the lower rather than the higher of two touching honour cards is led. Also called 'Rusinow' leads.

ROMAN SYSTEM
System devised by Walter Avarelli and Giorgio Belladonna and used by them as members of the Italian Blue Team. The system is based on an artificial 1♣ opening (either balanced 12–16 points or 17+ points) and canape. See CANAPE

ROMAN TWO DIAMOND CONVENTION
A convention whereby a 2◊ opening shows a strong three-suited hand with, typically, 17–20 high card points.

ROMEX TRIAL BIDS
A method of allowing a player to make both long-suit and short-suit trial bids, by employing relays after a single raise of a major suit.

ROPE
After a 4NT Ace enquiry is doubled, <u>R</u>edouble shows an <u>O</u>dd number of Aces, <u>P</u>ass an <u>E</u>ven number.

ROPI
After a 4NT Ace enquiry is doubled, <u>R</u>edouble shows zero (<u>O</u>) Aces, <u>P</u>ass one (<u>I</u>).

ROSENBLUM TROPHY
See WORLD CHAMPIONSHIPS

ROTATION
The sequence and order in which the bidding and play occur at the table.

ROUND
The number of boards in a duplicate event which a pair play against the same opposition.

ROUND OFF
To round off the net score at the end of a rubber to the nearest hundred, with most players rounding 50 downwards.

ROUND ROBIN
A form of contest in which each competing group (team, pair or individual) plays against every other competing group.

ROUNDED SUITS
Clubs and hearts, so named because of the shape of their symbols. Spades and diamonds are similarly called 'Pointed Suits'.

ROVER
An additional pair in a Mitchell movement which displaces a different North–South pair each round, known as a 'roving pair'.

RUBBER
The best of three games in rubber bridge. It is thought that the term 'rubber' is derived from the game of bowls.

RUBBER BRIDGE
The form of contract bridge in which the objective is to make two games before your opponents, and thereby win the rubber. A game can be achieved by scoring 100 points 'below the line' either on one deal, or by accumulating partscores to reach that total. See ABOVE THE LINE, BELOW THE LINE

RUBBER DUPLICATE
A teams-of-four event in which boards are played in a fixed order in both rooms until a rubber is reached in one room.

RUFF
To play a trump on the lead of a side suit.

RUFF AND DISCARD
To discard a loser from one hand while ruffing in the other.

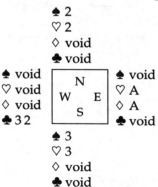

South is declarer and spades are trumps. If any hand other than

West is on lead then a heart must be lost. But with West on lead and obliged to lead a club, South can ruff in dummy and discard a heart from hand. Alternatively, he could choose to discard a heart from dummy and ruff in his own hand.

RUFFING FINESSE
The lead of one of a sequence of high cards towards a void. If the card is not covered, it is allowed to run; if it is covered, it can then be ruffed to establish winners. For example:

```
              K Q J 10
            ┌─────────┐
            │    N    │
   98762    │ W     E │  A 5 4 3
            │    S    │
            └─────────┘
               void
```

South, declarer, leads the King of a side-suit from dummy. If East plays his Ace, it is ruffed, thus establishing the Q J 10 as winners. If East plays low, South discards a loser.

RUFFING TRICK
A trick won by a ruff.

RULE OF ELEVEN
A simple mathematical formula which states that, if the fourth-highest card of a suit is led from one hand, then the number of cards capable of beating it in the other three hands is equal to eleven minus the pip value of the card led. For example:

```
                K 5 2
            ┌─────────┐
            │    N    │
            │ W     E │  7 led
            │    S    │
            └─────────┘
              A J 9 6 3
```

If East judges that the 7 is a fourth-highest lead, he can use the rule of eleven to deduce that South has no card higher than the 7 and hence that he may play low at trick One to leave West on lead to play a second round of the suit through dummy's King at trick Two.

RULE OF NINETEEN
Rule established by the Laws and Ethics Committee of the EBU, stating that the minimum agreeable standard for an opening suit bid at the one-level is that the sum of the number of high-card points and the lengths of the two longest suits must total at least nineteen. For example:

♠ K
♡ 86542
◇ AQ642
♣ 54

With 9 high-card points and two 5-card suits, this hand would be minimally acceptable under the Rule of Nineteen for an opening bid (9+5+5). Note that this Rule does not suggest that weak hands of this type justify a sensible opening bid, but rather that bidding with a lower total than 19 would constitute a psyche.

RULE OF TWO AND THREE
The doctrine, in pre-emptive bidding, that one should not risk going down more than two tricks, if vulnerable, and three tricks if not vulnerable.

RULING
A decision based upon the Laws of the game, made by a Tournament Director or by an Appeals Committee.

RUN
1 To change to a different suit or to No Trumps if a contract is doubled for penalties.
2 To run a suit is to play it card after card without losing the lead.
3 To take a finesse by leading an honour and play low if it is not covered. See RIDE

RUSINOW LEADS
See ROMAN LEADS

—S—

SACRIFICE

A bid made in the full expectation that the contract will be defeated, but in the hope that the points lost will be fewer than those that the opponents would have scored had they been left to play in their own contract.

SAFETY PLAY

A way of handling a suit combination to give the greatest chance of making the required number of tricks in the suit at the expense of abandoning the possibility of gaining extra tricks.

$$
\text{A K 9 6 4} \quad
\begin{array}{|c|}
\hline
\text{N} \\
\text{W} \quad \text{E} \\
\text{S} \\
\hline
\end{array}
\quad \text{J 7 3}
$$

Four tricks are required from the above holding. The 'Safety Play' is to cash the Ace and then lead low to the Jack.

SAVE

Used in the same sense as 'Sacrifice'. See SACRIFICE

SBU

See SCOTTISH BRIDGE UNION

SCHWAB TROPHY

See WORLD CHAMPIONSHIPS

SCISSORS COUP

A play used, as the name implies, to cut communications between the opposing hands usually to destroy an enemy entry needed to give his partner a ruff. For example:

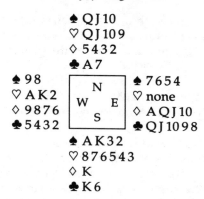

```
              ♠ Q J 10
              ♡ Q J 10 9
              ◇ 5 4 3 2
              ♣ A 7
  ♠ 98      ┌─────────┐   ♠ 7 6 5 4
  ♡ A K 2   │    N    │   ♡ none
  ◇ 9 8 7 6 │ W     E │   ◇ A Q J 10
  ♣ 5 4 3 2 │    S    │   ♣ Q J 10 9 8
            └─────────┘
              ♠ A K 3 2
              ♡ 8 7 6 5 4 3
              ◇ K
              ♣ K 6
```

South plays in 4♡. West leads the ♠9. At trick Two declarer must play a diamond to his King to snip communications between the opposing hands in order to stop the ruff in spades.

SCORE
1 The written result of a contract.
2 To obtain a good result on a board, e.g.'We scored well on board thirteen'.

SCORE CARD
A card for keeping a record and used to score in a teams event, or a personal record in a pairs or individual event. See PERSONAL SCORE CARD

SCORE SHEET
See RECAPITULATION SHEET

SCORESLIP
1 In rubber bridge or Chicago, printed paper or pad to record the score.
2 In duplicate, the traveller that accompanies the board.
See TRAVELLER OR TRAVELLING SCORESLIP

SCORING CORRECTIONS
An error in computing or tabulating the agreed score, whether

made by a player or a scorer, may be corrected within a timescale set by the sponsoring organisation. If no time is set then the period for correction is thirty minutes after the official score has been posted. See PROTEST PERIOD

SCOTTISH BRIDGE UNION
Regulatory body for Duplicate Bridge in Scotland.

SCRAMBLED MITCHELL
A method of producing a single winner from a Mitchell event by arrow switching the compass points of the pairs (on certain rounds). On such rounds the East–West pairs (and the boards) move normally, but they then play the North–South cards and vice versa. Generally the final one or two rounds are arrow switched in a scrambled movement. See MITCHELL

SCREEN
In major championships, a large screen is placed diagonally across the table preventing each player from being able to see his partner and one of his opponents. A small slit in the screen allows a tray to slide from one side of the table to the other. The auction is conducted, using bidding boxes, by placing the bids on this tray and repeatedly sliding it from one side of the table to the other. During the cardplay a flap is raised to allow just enough visibility for all players to see the dummy and the cards as they are played. The purpose of screens is to prevent players conveying information to their partners through their mannerisms or eye contact.

SCREEN-MATE
When screens are in use, he is the opponent seated on one's own side of the screen.

SECOND HAND LOW
A favourite maxim of whist play that, following the lead of a small card, the second hand to play to the trick should play his lowest card of the suit led.

SECONDARY SQUEEZE
A squeeze in which the opponents win one or more tricks after the squeeze card has been played:

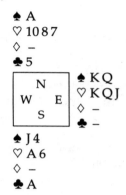

♠ A
♡ 10 8 7
◊ –
♣ 5

♠ K Q
♡ K Q J
◊ –
♣ –

♠ J 4
♡ A 6
◊ –
♣ A

When South plays ♣A, East will be limited to only a heart trick, whichever discard he chooses.

SECONDARY SUPPORT
A useful holding in a suit bid by partner, often a three-card suit as distinct from four-card (primary) support. See PRIMARY SUPPORT

SECTION
If a competition field is split into separate groups, each group is called a section.

SEMI-BALANCED
Hands with 5–4–2–2 or 6–3–2–2 shape.

SEMI-PSYCHIC
A 'semi-psychic' bid is one which, whilst it is made deliberately with the intention of confusing the opponents, nevertheless only slightly misdescribes the hand. Examples are the 'third-in-hand opener', or a No Trump bid, which is one or two points under strength.

SEMI-SOLID SUIT
A suit which is likely to have only one loser, for example: A Q J 10 8 4.

SEQUENCE
Cards in consecutive rank order, for example K Q J.

SEQUENCE DISCARDS
The discard of an honour guarantees the honour immediately below it and denies the honour immediately above it.

SESSION
A period of play during which a competitor is scheduled to play a given number of boards.

SET
1 To defeat a contract.
2 To set up a suit is to establish it.
3 Set of duplicate boards or wallets. There are usually 32 boards in a set.
4 A pre-arranged rubber bridge match played between two fixed partnerships.

SHADED
A bid is said to be shaded if it is slightly below the normal strength requirements.

SHAPE
The way in which the four suits are arranged within one hand. For example: 5–4–3–1 'shape.' This is also called the hand's 'pattern' or 'distribution'.

SHARING BOARDS
In some movements, it is necessary for two or more tables to play the same boards on the same round. This is called 'Sharing boards'. Boards may be played in a different sequence as a result.

SHARK
Colloquialism for an expert player, who specializes in playing rubber bridge for money, and who is particularly adept at this type of competition.

SHARPLES CONVENTION
A defence to 1NT whereby an overcall of 2♣ shows a hand of unspecified shape but with at least four spades and 2◇ shows a weak distributional hand with short clubs. See DEFENCE TO 1NT

SHIFT
1   In the auction, a change of suit as in 'Jump shift'.
2   In the play, a switch to another suit.

SHOOTING FOR A TOP
To make an apparently inferior bid or play in a deliberate attempt to score a top. The tactic is usually employed by a pair towards the end of a duplicate session in an attempt to convert a good score into a winning score.

SHORT CLUB
See PHONEY CLUB

SHORT HAND
The hand with the fewer number of cards in a suit (usually trumps).

SHORT SUIT GAME TRIES
A game try whereby, after trump agreement, opener shows his shortest suit and invites responder to judge accordingly.

SHORT SUIT LEADS
The lead of a short suit, usually when partner has bid the suit, but sometimes as a deceptive play hoping that declarer will think that the wrong hand has the long suit.

SHORTEN
To reduce in length. Commonly refers to the situation where

dummy's or declarer's trumps are removed by forcing him to ruff. See PUNCH

SHOW OUT
To reveal a void by discarding on the lead of a suit.

SHUFFLE
To mix the cards randomly.

SHUT-OUT BID
See PRE-EMPTIVE BID

SID
An acronym for **S**tayman **I**n **D**oubt. See STAYMAN IN DOUBT

SIDE
A partnership in a rubber game; a duplicate game or teams-of-four match.

SIDE GAME
A second competition at a championship for pairs or teams not involved in the main event.

SIDE SUIT
A suit other than trumps. It is also known as a 'plain suit'.

SIGN-OFF
A discouraging bid suggesting that the partnership should progress no further.

SIGNALS, SIGNALLING
The method of conveying information between the defenders. This can be done both when following to a suit and when discarding.

SILENT
To keep 'silent' is to pass throughout the auction.

SILENT BIDDER
See DUMB BIDDER, WRITTEN BIDDING

SIMPLE FINESSE
A finesse against one outstanding card.

SIMPLE OVERCALL
A non-jump overcall.

SIMULTANEOUS PAIRS
Event played in many different venues on the same date and with identical hands so that nationwide, or even worldwide match-pointing may be employed.

SINGLE-DUMMY PROBLEMS
Bridge problems presented as if in the position of declarer.

SINGLE RAISE
A raise of partner's denomination by one level.

SINGLETON
A holding of only one card in a suit.

SIT OUT
If there is an odd number of pairs in a duplicate event, one pair must sit out each round as it has no opponents. It also means to wait to cut in to a game of rubber bridge.

SKIP BID
See JUMP BID, STOP

SKIP BID WARNING
Sponsoring organisations require that a warning be given before a jump bid (skip bid) is made and require the next player to pause for a specified period before bidding. See STOP

SKIP ROUND
A round during a Mitchell movement at which the East–West

pairs 'skip', moving two tables instead of the usual one. The boards move as normal. See MITCHELL

SLAM
A contract for twelve tricks (Small Slam) or thirteen tricks (Grand Slam). For bidding and making either type of slam considerable bonuses are awarded. See BONUS

SLAM CONVENTION
An agreed bidding convention, such as Blackwood, for checking on controls, trumps or other key cards held by the partnership to investigate slam possibilities.

SLAM DOUBLES
See LIGHTNER DOUBLE, UNPENALTY DOUBLE

SLIDING BLACKWOOD
See ROLLING BLACKWOOD

SLIDING GERBER
See ROLLING GERBER

SLUFF
Slang term meaning to discard a loser.

SMALL CARD
In general a card below honour rank, often denoted by an 'x' on a hand record.

SMALL SLAM
To contract to make twelve tricks is to bid a Small Slam. It is sometimes called a 'Little Slam'. See BONUS

SMITH PETER
Against no trumps, on the lead of declarer's first suit, the partner of the opening leader plays high-low to show that he would like the suit to be continued if partner regains the lead. The opening leader plays high-low to show a poor holding in his suit. See ATTITUDE SIGNALS

SMOTHER PLAY

A rare endplay in which a seemingly certain losing trump trick vanishes. The defending hand with trump length is reduced to trumps alone and has the choice of underruffing, thus unguarding his honour, or overuffing only to be overruffed in turn. For example:

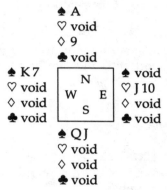

```
                ♠ A
                ♡ void
                ◊ 9
                ♣ void
   ♠ K 7     ┌──────────┐   ♠ void
   ♡ void    │    N     │   ♡ J 10
   ◊ void    │  W   E   │   ◊ void
   ♣ void    │    S     │   ♣ void
            └──────────┘
                ♠ Q J
                ♡ void
                ◊ void
                ♣ void
```

Spades are trumps and East, on lead, plays a heart. South, declarer, ruffs and West is subjected to a 'smother play' or coup.

SNAP

An acronym for **S**trong **N**o Trump **A**fter **P**assing, this convention uses the response of 1NT to an opening bid of one of a suit, made by partner third or fourth in hand, to show 8–10 points.

SOFT VALUES

Queens and Jacks. By comparison Aces and Kings are called 'hard values'.

SOLID

1 Describes a suit with no losers.
2 An unbeatable contract.

SOS REDOUBLE

A redouble suggesting that an alternative denomination be chosen from the one which has been doubled.

SOUTH
One of the positions at the bridge table.

SOUTH AFRICAN TEXAS
The use of 4♣ and 4◇ bids as transfers to 4♡ and 4♠ respectively, either as opening bids or in response to 1NT/2NT. The transfer to 4♡ suggests a stronger hand than bidding 4♡ directly.

SPLINTER BID
A double jump response, usually to a major-suit opening, showing trump support, the values for game, and a singleton or void in the suit bid.

SPLIT
The way a suit is divided.

SPLITTING HONOURS
The play of an honour, from two or more in sequence, in the second position. For example:

```
              A J 4
            ┌───────┐
            │   N   │
    K Q 9   │ W   E │   10 8 3 2
            │   S   │
            └───────┘
              7 6 5
```

South leads the 5 and, if West plays the King or Queen, he is said to 'split his honours'.

SPOT CARDS
Cards from the 2 to the 9 inclusive.

SPREAD
1 To place the cards of the dummy face up on the table.
2 To lay one's hand on the table in making a claim.
3 A term for an unbeatable contract as in 'Four spades was a spread'.

SPUTNIK DOUBLE
See NEGATIVE DOUBLE

SQUEEZE
Descriptive term for a variety of plays where an opponent is forced to discard in a suit or suits that he wishes to guard. The end result is that the enemy makes a trick (sometimes more) that seemed unlikely at the start of play. There are a great many squeeze plays, many with set names, varying from the simple to the complex. Here are two basic ones:

1a)

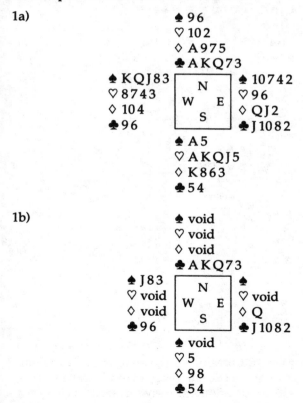

```
                    ♠ 96
                    ♡ 10 2
                    ◇ A975
                    ♣ AKQ73
    ♠ KQJ83    ┌─────────┐   ♠ 10742
    ♡ 8743     │    N    │   ♡ 96
    ◇ 104      │  W   E  │   ◇ QJ2
    ♣ 96       │    S    │   ♣ J1082
               └─────────┘
                    ♠ A5
                    ♡ AKQJ5
                    ◇ K863
                    ♣ 54
```

1b)

```
                    ♠ void
                    ♡ void
                    ◇ void
                    ♣ AKQ73
    ♠ J83      ┌─────────┐   ♠
    ♡ void     │    N    │   ♡ void
    ◇ void     │  W   E  │   ◇ Q
    ♣ 96       │    S    │   ♣ J1082
               └─────────┘
                    ♠ void
                    ♡ 5
                    ◇ 98
                    ♣ 54
```

South can make 6♣ or 6♡ without problem, but he goes for a top score by playing in 6NT, and gets ♠K lead. He ducks the first spade (see RECTIFYING THE COUNT) and wins the continuation. Then he cashes ◊A K and plays off from his hearts reaching the position in 1b) . When the ♡5 is played, East becomes simply squeezed and must unguard one of his minor suits. This is known as a 'simple squeeze'.

2a)

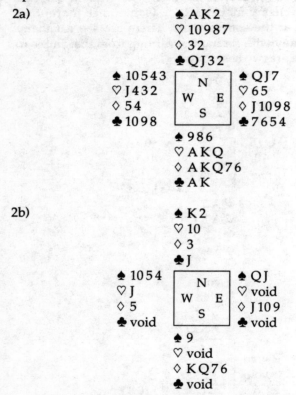

2b)

South plays in 7NT and West leads the ♣10 There are twelve top tricks and if either red suit breaks 3–3 there will be no problem. The heart suit fails to work but South gives himself an extra chance by arriving in position 2b). East has already discarded a club on a heart and, when North's ♣J is led, must discard a spade. South throws a diamond. When South now wins ◊K Q, West must either discard a spade or a heart. Either is fatal and both opponents have been squeezed. See ALTERNATIVE, AUTOMATIC, COMPOUND, COUNT, CRISS-CROSS, DOUBLE, GUARD, HEXAGON, POSITIONAL, PROGRESSIVE, SECONDARY, SUICIDE, TRANSFER, TRIPLE

SQUEEZE WITHOUT THE COUNT
Term used for a squeeze which can be executed without the requirement to rectify the count. See RECTIFYING THE COUNT

STACKED
The cards are said to be 'stacked' against one, when a single opponent holds all or nearly all the crucial cards in a given suit.

STAKES
Rubber bridge is usually played for 'stakes'. Although it is a social game, the addition of a substantial, or even nominal stake provides an incentive to bid and play carefully and accurately.

STAND A DOUBLE
To pass partner's double.

STAND UP
A card is said to 'stand up' if it wins a trick.

STANDARD AMERICAN
Nebulous term for bidding methods commonly used in America, approximately those that were originally laid down by Charles H. Goren.

STANDARD HONOUR LEADS
See LEADING FROM HONOURS

STANZA
A set of boards played before scoring or moving to another table.

STAYMAN CONVENTION
A 2♣ response to a 1NT opening bid, used to enquire about major

suit holdings. In response, opener rebids:

2◊   No four card major
2♡   Four hearts (and possibly four spades)
2♠   Four spades

See STAYMAN THREE CLUBS

STAYMAN IN DOUBT (SID)

After a positive response to the 2♣ enquiry (2♠/2♡), a bid of 3◊ indicates a four-card fit in the bid major, values for game but a 4–3–3–3 or 3–4–3–3 hand pattern. Partner chooses either to bid four of the major or 3NT depending on his hand pattern. Duplication of distribution may mean that 3NT is an easier game contract despite the 4–4 major suit fit.

STAYMAN THREE CLUBS

The use of 3♣ in response to a 2NT opening to enquire about four-card majors in the same way that 2♣ is used in response to 1NT.

STEP RESPONSES

System of responses, especially to an artificial bid such as a Blackwood 4NT enquiry, whereby the number of features (Aces, controls, points etc.) is shown by steps.

STIFF

Singleton, usually a high honour card, as in 'The stiff King'.

STOP

A method of alerting the opponents that a player is about to make a jump bid. The player who is about to make such a jump bid precedes his bid with the words 'Stop' or 'Skip bid'. The next player should then pause for about ten seconds before bidding.

STOPPER (A STOP)

A holding that prevents the immediate run of a suit.

STRIP PLAY

To strip a player of safe exit cards, so that when the defender is thrown in he cannot avoid conceding a trick.

STRIPED-TAILED APE DOUBLE
A double of a game (or slam) contract in the expectation that the opponents could make a Small Slam (or Grand Slam) and in the hope that they will accept the apparently good score for making a doubled game (or slam) with overtricks rather than go on to the higher-scoring slam. The convention is so named because the doubler flees like a 'striped-tailed ape' in the face of a redouble.

STRONG JUMP OVERCALLS
A single jump overcall showing a good six-card suit and about 15–17 high card points.

STRONG KINGS AND TENS
A system of honour leads against a No Trump contract whereby the lead of a King or 10 suggests a strong holding, and the lead of an Ace, Queen or Jack suggests a relatively weak holding.

Ace from:	A K x
King from:	A K Q, A K J, A K 10, K Q J, K Q 10
Queen from:	K Q x, K Q 9, Q J 10
Jack from:	J 10 x
Ten from:	A J 10, A 10 9, K J 10, K 10 9, Q 10 9
Nine from:	10 9 x

STRONG MINOR RAISE
See INVERTED MINOR SUIT RAISES

STRONG NO TRUMP
An opening 1NT bid with usually 15–17 or 16–18 points and a balanced hand.

STRONG NO TRUMP AFTER PASSING
See SNAP

STRONG PASS SYSTEMS
Systems featuring an opening pass in first or second position to show about 16+ points.

STRONG TWO BID
An opening bid of two of a suit used to show a strong hand with at least five cards in the suit named. They may be played as not forcing, forcing for one round or forcing to game. See ACOL TWO BID, FORCING TWO BID

SUCKERS DOUBLE
A double of a freely-bid game or slam contract by a player who is relying solely on defensive high-card strength. Against good opponents, such doubles can result in an 'unmakeable' contract being made. It is probable that the declaring side has distributional values to compensate for missing high-card values.

SUFFICIENT BID
A bid at a higher level than the previous bid or at the same level in a higher-ranking denomination.

SUICIDE SQUEEZE
A squeeze when a defender, rather than declarer, leads the card that inflicts the squeeze.

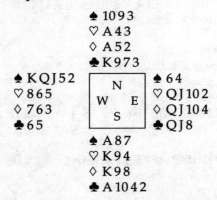

```
                    ♠ 10 9 3
                    ♡ A 4 3
                    ◇ A 5 2
                    ♣ K 9 7 3
     ♠ K Q J 5 2    ┌─────────┐    ♠ 6 4
     ♡ 8 6 5        │    N    │    ♡ Q J 10 2
     ◇ 7 6 3        │ W     E │    ◇ Q J 10 4
     ♣ 6 5          │    S    │    ♣ Q J 8
                    └─────────┘
                    ♠ A 8 7
                    ♡ K 9 4
                    ◇ K 9 8
                    ♣ A 10 4 2
```

West leads top spades against South's 3NT. With only eight apparent tricks available, South wins the second round and plays a third spade. Now West has no option but to cash his remaining spade winners, with the last of which he 'suicidally' squeezes his partner into unguarding one of his suits.

SUIT
Method of categorizing the fifty-two cards in a pack, identified by the shape of the pip, spades, hearts, diamonds or clubs.

SUIT PREFERENCE SIGNAL
Defensive signal whereby the play of the cards in one suit is used to indicate preference between two other suits. See McKENNEY, REVOLVING DISCARDS

SUPPORT
1 To raise partner's suit.
2 A worthwhile holding in partner's suit.

SUPPRESSING THE BID ACE
To ignore an already identified Ace (such as by a cue bid) in responding to Blackwood.

SURE TRICK
A trick that a player is certain to make.

SWING
The net difference in the score on a board in a teams match.

SWING HAND
A hand on which a large swing in scores occurred, or which had the potential for a large swing.

SWISS CONVENTION
A convention whereby responses of 4♣ or 4◇ to an opening of one of a major show a good fit, sound values for game and some interest in a slam, thus releasing the direct raise to four of opener's major to be used pre-emptively. There are many versions of Swiss. The three most popular are:

Singleton Swiss
4♣ Shows two Aces and a singleton. 4◇ from partner asks responder to identify the singleton
4◇ Shows two Aces without a singleton

Fruit machine Swiss (Three-way Swiss)

4♣   Shows either two Aces and a singleton, or three Aces, or two Aces and the King of trumps. 4◊ from opener is then a relay requesting clarification. In reply, 4NT shows three Aces, a bid of four of the agreed trump suit shows two Aces and the trump King, and a new suit shows two Aces and a singleton in the suit bid

4◊   Shows two Aces without any of the features shown by the 4♣ response

Trump Swiss

4♣   Shows good controls
4◊   Shows good trumps

More complex versions of Swiss (e.g. Super Swiss) use conventional responses of 3NT and a double jump in the unbid major in addition to the responses of 4♣ and 4◊. In conjunction with further relays they allow responder to make very fine distinctions between different types of raises. See MINOR SUIT SWISS

SWISS PAIRS

A pairs competition where instead of using a fixed Movement the scores are calculated at the end of each round and pairs are drawn against others with similar scores for the next round.

SWISS TEAMS

A competition for teams organized in the same way as for Swiss Pairs.

SWITCH

1   To lead a different suit from the one previously being led.
2   Arrow-switch, an adaptation towards the end of a session allowing a single winner to be determined from a Mitchell movement.
See MITCHELL, SCRAMBLED MITCHELL

SYSTEM

The methods of bidding and cardplay used by a partnership.

—T—

TABLE
1 A team of four, two pairs or four players in a duplicate event.
2 The dummy.
3 To 'table' one's hand it to expose it, either as dummy or when making a claim.

TABLE NUMBERS
Numbered cards placed on each table for identification purposes.

TABLE PRESENCE
The almost indefinable characteristic possessed by expert players whereby they draw correct inferences from their opponents' mannerisms and rhythm of play etc.

TACTICS
General manoeuvres in bidding and play, and other choices of action in adapting one's rubber bridge style to the peculiarities of tournament play. Different methods of scoring and conditions of contest often determine that a modified approach to the game be adopted.

TAKE OUT
A bid in a denomination other than that previously bid by partner. See WEAKNESS TAKE OUT

TAKE-OUT DOUBLE
A double which is used conventionally to ask partner to bid his best suit. Traditionally a double is defined as being for take-out if it is:
1 Of a suit bid at the one- or two-level.
2 Made at the first opportunity to double that suit.
3 Made before partner has bid.

TANK, TO GO INTO THE
To pause for a long time when faced with a difficult decision in bidding or play.

TAP
To gently knock the table:
1 A method of alerting partner's conventional bid.
2 In rubber bridge, to pass.

TARTAN TWO BIDS
Opening bids of 2♡ and 2♠ to show a variety of types of hand. 2♡ shows either a weak hand (about 5–9 points) with five hearts and a five-card minor, or an Acol 2♡ opener, or a strong balanced hand (about 19/20 points). 2♠ shows either a weak hand (about 5–9 points) with five spades and another five-card suit, or an Acol 2♠ opener. After both openings a response in the next available bid is used as a relay to seek clarification.

TEAM
A group of four or more players competing as a single unit.

TEMPO
1 To have the initiative in the play. For example:

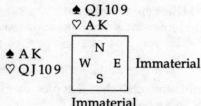

West on lead against South's No Trump contract has the initiative (tempo) and can guarantee four tricks by leading his long suit.
2 In bidding or play, the general rhythm of a player's actions.

TEMPORIZING BID
See WAITING BID

TENACE
A holding of two (normally high) cards in the same suit, one

ranking next above and the other next below a card held by an opponent, e.g. A Q or K J. A holding which is not strictly a tenace before play starts may become one during the course of play. For example A J x opposite x x x becomes a tenace if the King is led. See MAJOR TENACE, MINOR TENACE

TEXAS CONVENTION
A transfer method in response to a 1NT/2NT opening bid. In response, a jump to 4◊ is a transfer to 4♡ and a bid of 4♡ a transfer to 4♠. See SOUTH AFRICAN TEXAS

THIN
1   A contract bid on very slender values.
2   A hand too weak for a specific action.

THIRD AND FIFTH LEADS
A convention whereby, from long suits without an honour sequence, the third highest card is led from three- and four-card suits and the fifth highest is led from longer holdings.

THIRD HAND HIGH
A whist rule suggesting that the correct action to take when one's partner has led is to play one's highest card (but the lowest of equals).

THIRD-IN-HAND OPENER
In the third seat it can be good tactics to open on a hand that is slightly below the usual strength for an opening bid. Such an opening is called a 'third-in-hand' opener, and it may be termed as semi-psychic.

THREAT CARD (MENACE)
A card which, whilst not yet a winner, may become established as a winner if the opponents can be forced to weaken their holding in the suit. The term is principally used in connection with squeezes. See SQUEEZE

THREE-HANDED BRIDGE
There are many versions of this game, which is popularly known as 'cut-throat bridge'. Usually the three players bid against each other for the dummy, which may be kept face down, or have a number of cards exposed during the auction.

THREE NO TRUMP FOR TAKE-OUT
A convention whereby an overcall of 3NT after an opponent's three-level pre-emptive opening is a take-out request. See DEFENCE TO OPENING THREE BID

THREE-QUARTER MOVEMENT
An incomplete Howell movement when not all the pairs meet. See HOWELL

THREE-QUARTER NO TRUMP
To play a strong No Trump only when vulnerable against non-vulnerable opponents, with a weak No Trump at other times.

THREE-SUITER
A hand with four or more cards in three suits i.e. 4–4–4–1 or 5–4–4–0.

THROUGH STRENGTH
See LEAD THROUGH STRENGTH

THROW AWAY
To discard.

THROW IN
1 A deal when all four players pass.
2 To give a player the lead deliberately, with the expectation of a favourable return. See ENDPLAY

TIGHT
A contract close to failure.

TOP
Highest matchpoint score available on each board in a duplicate pairs event.

TOP OF NOTHING
Standard lead with a holding of two or three small cards (and sometimes more).

TOTAL POINT SCORING
Form of scoring at teams whereby the team with the largest aggregate score wins.

TOUCHING CARDS
Cards in sequence.

TOUCHING SUITS
Clubs and diamonds, diamonds and hearts, hearts and spades and spades and clubs are said to be touching suits.

TOURNAMENT DIRECTOR
Person delegated by the sponsoring organization to see to the smooth running of the tournament, to give rulings on points of law and to sort out any irregularities.

TOURNAMENT DIRECTOR'S GUIDE
Book of advice for Tournament Directors, intended as an explanatory supplement to the Laws and as a guide to their implementation. See LAWS OF DUPLICATE CONTRACT BRIDGE

TRAM TICKETS
Very poor cards.

TRANCE
To pause for a substantial length of time during bidding or play.

TRANSFER BIDS
Bids of suits which show the suit ranking immediately above that

which is bid, and command partner to bid that suit. They are most commonly used after partner opens 1NT or 2NT and allow greater flexibility in the bidding. The basic principle is that with, for example, a five-card or longer heart suit, one responds in diamonds. Partner will convert to hearts after which responder may pass with a weak hand, or make some further descriptive bid. An elaborate system of 'transfer bidding' sequences can be used to describe a range of hand-types. See JACOBY TRANSFERS

TRANSFER SQUEEZE

A squeeze play which results from transferring the menace. For example:

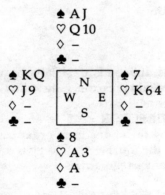

```
              ♠ A J
              ♡ Q 10
              ◇ –
              ♣ –
    ♠ K Q    ┌───────┐    ♠ 7
    ♡ J 9    │   N   │    ♡ K 6 4
    ◇ –      │ W   E │    ◇ –
    ♣ –      │   S   │    ♣ –
             └───────┘
              ♠ 8
              ♡ A 3
              ◇ A
              ♣ –
```

Both North and South have menaces in two suits, but, if North is on lead, each opponent controls one of the menaces and neither can be squeezed. If, however, the ♡Q is led (covered by the King and Ace), the menace is 'transferred' to the South hand. The lead of ◇A will catch West in a Guard Squeeze immediately.

TRANSFERRING THE MENACE

Method of changing which opponent guards a particular suit, in order that a squeeze can be executed. See SQUEEZE, THREAT CARD (MENACE)

TRAP PASS
To pass holding a strong hand in the hope the opposition will overbid and a good penalty can be extracted.

TRAVELLER OR TRAVELLING SCORESLIP
The slip of paper which accompanies a board as it travels round the room in a duplicate event, on which the result of each pair that has played played the hand is recorded.

TREATMENT
That part of an agreed system designed to handle certain situations that arise in the bidding. It may also be a variation of a particular convention.

TRIAL BID
A bid in a new suit when trumps have been agreed which invites partner to bid game if he is good for his previous bidding but allows room for him to sign off in a partscore if he is poor. With halfway values he should refer to his holding in the 'trial bid' suit. See SHORT SUIT GAME TRIES

TRICK
The lead, and three subsequent cards played in rotation.

TRICK POINTS
Points recorded below the line in rubber bridge.

TRIPLE RAISE
A raise missing out two levels of bidding. It is usually pre-emptive in nature.

TRIPLE SQUEEZE
A squeeze against one opponent in three suits. For example:

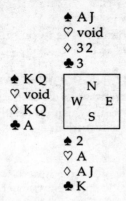

```
              ♠ A J
              ♡ void
              ◊ 3 2
              ♣ 3
♠ K Q        ┌─────────┐
♡ void       │    N    │
◊ K Q        │ W     E │
♣ A          │    S    │
             └─────────┘
              ♠ 2
              ♡ A
              ◊ A J
              ♣ K
```

When South leads the ♡A West is squeezed in three suits. Indeed he must throw a spade in order to avoid a being squeezed again.

TRIPLETON
A holding of three cards in a suit.

TRUMP
A card in the trump suit as determined by the last suit bid in the auction.

TRUMP ASKING BID
A bid which enquires as to the quality of partner's trump holding. See ASKING BID, GRAND SLAM FORCE

TRUMP CONTROL
The player with the longest trump holding in one hand is said to have trump control. When two players have equally long trump suits then the player whose partnership has the lead has the tempo and therefore trump control. See TEMPO

TRUMP COUP
A stratagem whereby an opponent's finessable trumps are trapped without an actual finesse being taken. For example:

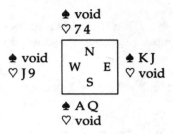

```
            ♠ void
            ♡ 7 4
                  N
  ♠ void     W       E    ♠ K J
  ♡ J 9          S         ♡ void

            ♠ A Q
            ♡ void
```

With spades as trumps, South, declarer, leads a heart from dummy. See GRAND COUP

TRUMP ECHO

A high-low signal in the trump suit. This is usually used either to give count in the trump suit (an 'echo' showing an odd number, particularly three, when playing standard signals) and to indicate an interest in obtaining a ruff.

TRUMP KING

Often regarded as a 'fifth' Ace in control-showing bids.

TRUMP PETER

See TRUMP ECHO

TRUMP PROMOTION

To promote a trump trick in a defender's hand. This can occur basically in two ways:

1 A plain suit card is led through declarer, allowing partner to make an extra trump trick. See COUP EN PASSANT
2 A defender ruffs with a high trump, forcing declarer to overruff higher thus promoting a trump trick for partner. See UPPERCUT

TRUMP REDUCTION PLAY

Play designed to reduce the number of trumps held by ruffing, usually in preparation for a trump coup or endplay.

TRUMP SIGNAL
An agreed method by defenders, when following in trumps, to show information in that suit or another suit. See TRUMP ECHO

TRUMP SUIT
The denomination of the last suit bid in the auction.

TRUMP SUPPORT
Support for partner in his proposed trump suit.

TRUSCOTT CONVENTION
Defence mechanism against strong (16+pts) artificial opening bids of 1♣ (as in Precision and Blue Club systems). The principle is to counter honour-point strength with distributional values. An overcall shows a two-suited hand with at least 5–4 distribution in the suits pinpointed by the following bids over 1♣.

1◇	shows diamonds and hearts
1♡	shows hearts and spades
1♠	shows spades and clubs
2♣	shows clubs and diamonds
1NT	shows diamonds and spades
Double	shows clubs and hearts.

TWO CLUB SYSTEMS
Systems employing a strong and forcing 2♣ opening bid.

TWO NO TRUMP OVERCALL
A balanced hand of some defined strength, but frequently played as a conventional bid. See UNUSUAL NO TRUMP

TWO OVER ONE
To respond, without jumping, to partner's one-level opening bid at the two-level. The bid shows greater values than are required for a one-level response.

TWO-SUITED OVERCALLS
Conventional overcalls which show two suits, at least one of which is specified.

TWO-SUITER
A hand with at least five cards in each of two suits.

TWO-WAY FINESSE
A card combination allowing declarer to finesse either opponent for a missing honour. For example:

K 10 6 A J 8

With the above card combination, declarer has the choice of finessing either opponent for the missing Queen.

TWO WAY STAYMAN
The use of 2♣ as a non-forcing Stayman and 2◊ as game-forcing Stayman. See STAYMAN CONVENTION

—U—

UNASSUMING CUE BID
The use of a cue bid in the opponent's suit, in response to an overcall by partner, to show at least a sound minimum raise of partner's suit, thus releasing direct raises to be used competitively or pre-emptively.

UNAUTHORIZED INFORMATION
Information available to a player which he is ethically bound to ignore. For example, an inference drawn from a hesitation by partner is 'unauthorized information', although, of course, it is perfectly legal to act upon an inference drawn from a hesitation by an opponent.

UNBALANCED DISTRIBUTION
Distribution which is not one of the balanced or semi-balanced hand patterns. An unbalance distribution will contain at least one singleton or void, in addition to one or more long suits.

UNBID SUIT
A suit not bid during the auction.

UNBLOCKING
The play of an unnecessarily high card in a suit to preserve a small card. For example:

$$AKJ32 \quad \begin{array}{c} \text{N} \\ \text{W} \quad \text{E} \\ \text{S} \end{array} \quad Q54$$

If West leads the Ace followed by the King, East must unblock the Queen in order that West can run the suit.

UNDER
To be under another player is to be on his right: e.g. West is under North.

UNDERBID
To make a bid suggesting a weaker hand than that actually held.

UNDERBIDDER
One who frequently underbids.

UNDERLEAD
To lead a small card from a holding including a high card.

UNDERRUFF
To discard a small trump under the ruffing card of an opponent. This unusual play may be to avoid being endplayed or simply because a discard in a side suit cannot be afforded.

UNDERTRICK
Each trick by which declarer fails in his contract.

UNLIMITED BID
A bid (such as the Acol 2♣ opener) with no upper limit.

UNPENALTY DOUBLE
A conventional double of a slam contract showing no defensive tricks, thus allowing partner to judge whether to sacrifice. With one or more defensive tricks, one should pass.

UNUSUAL NO TRUMP
A convention whereby an overall in No Trumps which, given the previous bidding, could not logically be natural, is used instead to show length in the two lowest-ranking unbid suits. The most popular application is as an immediate overcall of a suit opening, although this is an extension of the convention, for such a bid could logically be natural.

UP THE LINE
In ascending consecutive rank order, as in 'To bid four-card suits up the line'.

UP TO STRENGTH
1 In the auction, having full values for a bid.
2 In the play, the opposite of leading up to weakness.
See LEAD UP TO WEAKNESS

UP TO WEAKNESS
See LEAD UP TO WEAKNESS

UPPERCUT
To ruff high in order to try to promote a trump trick for partner. For example:

```
              ♠ 5 4 3
            ┌─────────┐
            │    N    │
  ♠ J 6     │ W     E │   ♠ Q 2
            │    S    │
            └─────────┘
            ♠ A K 10 9 8 7
```

With spades as trumps, West leads a suit in which both East and South are void and East ruffs with the Queen of spades. Assuming South overruffs, West's Jack is promoted.

UPSIDE DOWN SIGNALS/DISCARDS
See REVERSE SIGNALS/DISCARDS

UTILITY CLUB
See PHONEY CLUB

—V—

VANDERBILT, Harold Stirling
Developed contract bridge from auction bridge.

VANDERBILT TROPHY
See WORLD CHAMPIONSHIPS

VARIABLE NO TRUMP
An opening 1NT bid being weak when not vulnerable and strong when vulnerable.

VENICE CUP
See WORLD CHAMPIONSHIPS

VICTORY POINTS
In some events, usually teams competitions with International Matchpoint Scoring, a further conversion is made from Matchpoints to Victory Points. The conversion is made on a match by match basis. The purpose is to allow large victories to be rewarded more generously than small ones but to limit the extent of very large wins to prevent the result in one match effectively determining the outcome of an entire tournament.

VIENNA COUP
Unblocking play required when a menace is blocked and entries are lacking. A winning card in an opponent's suit is temporarily established, only for it to be lost in a squeeze. The play was first described by James Clay of London, a leading whist authority in the last century. He ascribed its discovery to the best whist player in Vienna, hence its name.

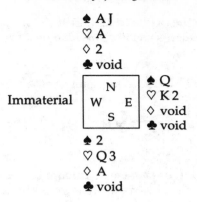

```
              ♠ A J
              ♡ A
              ◇ 2
              ♣ void
                                    ♠ Q
                     N              ♡ K 2
Immaterial    W         E           ◇ void
                     S              ♣ void
              ♠ 2
              ♡ Q 3
              ◇ A
              ♣ void
```

In this end position, the heart menace is blocked, thus North's heart Ace must be cashed before the diamond is led to squeeze East. See SQUEEZE

VIEW, TO TAKE A
To make a decision concerning the play or a bid.

VOID
A holding of no cards in a suit. See CHICHANE

VOID SHOWING BIDS
The use of an unusual jump to show a void in a side suit has found a place in many of the modern systems. In some methods no distinction is made initially between voids and singletons. It is possible to show a void in responding to a Blackwood enquiry of 4NT by making the normal response one level higher than usual, for example a 6◇ response showing one Ace and a working void. Another method involves specifying which void is held, by jumping to the suit below the trump suit with a low-ranking void and six of the trump suit with a high-ranking void. See CUE BID, SPLINTER BID

VUGRAPH
Theatre-style presentation of a hand of bridge as it is played using overhead projectors, closed circuit cameras etc, thus enabling an

audience to follow the play in detail. In addition to the presentation itself, commentary is usually provided by a panel of experts.

VULNERABLE
Term used to describe a side with a game. See AMBER, RED

—W—

WAITING BID
A non-committal bid, often a cheap forcing bid offering partner more time to describe his hand. It is sometimes known as a 'Temporizing bid'.

WALLET
Device used to hold cards while being moved in a duplicate event.

WBF
See WORLD BRIDGE FEDERATION

WBU
See WELSH BRIDGE UNION

WEAK FOUR BIDS
An opening bid at the four-level made with pre-emptive intent. See PRE-EMPTIVE OR SHUT OUT BID, RULE OF TWO AND THREE

WEAK JUMP OVERCALL
A jump overcall based on a six card suit and about 6–10 points.

WEAK JUMP SHIFT RESPONSES
The use of a jump shift in response to an opening bid of one of a suit to show a weak hand.

WEAK NO TRUMP
An opening bid of 1NT showing 12–14 points and a balanced hand.

WEAK THREE BIDS

An opening bid at the three-level made with pre-emptive intent. See PRE-EMPTIVE OR SHUT-OUT BID, RULE OF TWO AND THREE

WEAK TWO BIDS

An opening bid at the two-level, usually in the majors, with mainly preemptive intent. Typically such a bid is based on a six-card suit and 5–9 or 6–10 points. A 2NT response is usually used as an artificial response to enquiry about strength, suit quality, outside features or some combination of these. See BENJAMI-NISED ACOL (BENJAMIN CONVENTION)

WEAKNESS TAKE-OUT (WEAK TAKE-OUT)

A natural response, especially to an opening 1NT, which does not promise any strength, but merely expresses the wish to play in an alternative denomination.

WELSH BRIDGE UNION

Regulatory body for Duplicate Bridge in Wales.

WEST

One of the positions at the bridge table.

WHITE

Shorthand for describing the vulnerability of both partnerships on a board and meaning that neither partnership is vulnerable. See GREEN, AMBER, RED

WIDE OPEN

A player is said to have a suit 'wide open' if he has no guard in that suit in a No Trump contract, or no control in that suit in a slam contract.

WITHDRAWING A CARD

Permitted in correcting a revoke before it becomes established, or by an opponent following the correction of a revoke, or following

a revoke on the twelfth trick and in certain other defined situations
permitted by the Laws.

WORKING CARD
A card is said to be working if it is particularly useful, such as a
King or Queen in a suit bid by partner.

WORKING VOID
A void is said to be 'working' if it is particularly useful. This is
especially the case in slam bidding when a 'working void' is one in
which partner does not hold the ace.

WORLD BRIDGE FEDERATION (WBF)
The successor to the International Bridge League, the World
Bridge Federation was founded in 1958 to provide a global
organisation mainly to set uniform international standards for the
Laws of the game and to conduct World Bridge Championships.

WORLD CHAMPIONSHIPS
There are several World Championships:

Teams Olympiad
This is contested every four years. Entry is open to every country
(affiliated to the WBF) who may enter one team in each category,
the Open and the Ladies. The winners of the Open category
receive the Vanderbilt Trophy.

Bermuda Bowl
This is contested every two years. Entry is open to the open
champions of every WBF zone (approximately every continent).
In recent years the bigger zones have been allowed to enter more
than one team.

Venice Cup
This is contested every two years. Entry is open to the ladies
champions of every WBF zone (approximately every continent).
In recent years the bigger zones have been allowed to enter more
than one team.

Pairs Olympiad
This is contested every four years. Entry is open to every country (affiliated to the WBF) who may enter several pairs in each category, the number depending on the size of the country. There are three categories – Open, Ladies and Mixed. The winners of the open receive the Schwab Trophy (which was originally presented to the winners of a challenge match played in 1933 between Great Britain and the USA). In recent years a teams championship has been conducted in parallel with the pairs events, the winners receiving the Rosenblum Trophy. In 1990 the event was retitled a World Championship and three other world titles were introduced – Junior, Senior and Continuous Pairs, the last being open to anyone eliminated from the other championships.

WRIGGLE .
A convention whereby after an opening 1NT bid has been doubled, the responder with a weak hand attempts to locate a fit which will hopefully prove less costly than standing the double. A redouble shows clubs and another suit. A bid of 2♣ shows either clubs or a two-suited hand without clubs. Other responses are natural weakness take-out bids.

WRITTEN BIDDING
The use of a paper pad to record bids. Instead of making their bids vocally, players write them on a pad which is passed to each other. See SCREEN

X
1　Symbol used in recording hands when the x denotes a small card.
2　Symbol used when writing down a contract to denote that it is doubled (for example 4 ♡ x). Similarly two symbols denote that it is doubled and redoubled (for example 4 ♡ x x).

—Y—

YARBOROUGH
A hand containing no card higher than a nine, named after the English Lord who offered odds of a shilling to 100 guineas against holding such a hand (the true odds are 1827 to 1).

—Z—

ZERO
Lowest score possible on a board at duplicate. See BOTTOM